Secret
Loves

OTHER BOOKS BY DR. SONYA FRIEDMAN

Men Are Just Desserts
*How Learning to Be a Woman with a Life of Your Own Can Enrich the
Life You Share with a Man*

Smart Cookies Don't Crumble
A Modern Woman's Guide to Living and Loving Her Own Life

A Hero Is More than Just a Sandwich
How to Give Up Junk Food Love and Find a Naturally Sweet Man

On a Clear Day You Can See Yourself
Turning the Life You Have into the Life You Want

Secret Loves

WOMEN
WITH
TWO
LIVES

SONYA FRIEDMAN, PH.D.,

WITH

SONDRA FORSYTH

Crown Publishers, Inc.
New York

The stories in this book are true and were told to me by the women involved. Their names and all identifying characteristics have been changed to protect their privacy. Any resemblance to actual persons, living or dead, is entirely coincidental.

Grateful acknowledgment is made for permission to reprint three lines from "Dream Deferred" by Langston Hughes, from THE PANTHER AND THE LASH. Copyright 1951 by Langston Hughes. Reprinted by permission of Alfred A. Knopf, Inc.

Published by Crown Publishers, Inc., 201 East 50th Street, New York, New York 10022. Member of the Crown Publishing Group.

Random House, Inc.   New York, Toronto, London, Sydney, Auckland

CROWN is a trademark of Crown Publishers, Inc.

Manufactured in the United States of America

Design by Jennifer Harper

Library of Congress Cataloging-in-Publication Data
Friedman, Sonya.
    Secret loves: women with two lives / Sonya Friedman, Ph.D.,
with Sondra Forsyth. — 1st ed.
        p.   cm.
    Includes bibliographical references.
    1. Adultery—United States.   2. Man-woman relationships—United
States.   I. Forsyth, Sondra.   II. Title.
HQ806.F73   1994
306.73'6—dc20   93-22143
                                                                   CIP

ISBN 0-517-59052-2

10 9 8 7 6 5 4 3 2 1

First Edition

This book is dedicated to women all over the world who, unaware of their own power, resist recognizing it and who, sadly, continue to seek the approval of those who do recognize it, fear it, and devote their lives to supressing it.

Contents

Acknowledgments

*H*ow do you acknowledge people whose names you promised never to speak? How can I possibly thank more than one hundred women who came to dinner at my home or met me in restaurants and hotel lobbies around the country and cried and laughed and told me everything? All I can do is hope that I have served them well by allowing their struggle to live with their consciences as well as their needs to come through in an honest way. I honor their forthrightness and their trust of my commitment not to disclose anything that could directly identify them and in any way be destructive to their lives. Thank you for telling me your stories.

Sondra Forsyth, my collaborator, I reclaimed from my past life, when she was my editor at *Ladies' Home Journal*. There is no way this book could have been true to the stories the women told me without her. Her ability to capture their lives while transporting them to different settings was critical. She succeeded magnificently.

Loretta Barrett, my literary agent, is a gem. Supportive, kind, and authentic, she makes you believe, if you are the least bit unsure, that there really is a God.

Eileen Knipp, my administrative assistant, found herself acting as a researcher, a typist, a copy editor, and more as I tested her patience daily during this process.

Betty Prashker and Jane Meara, my editors at Crown, were unfailingly enthusiastic and encouraging. They offered expert guidance along the way, but most important, they respected my instincts and allowed me the freedom to shape and reshape the manuscript as the book began to take on a life of its own.

To family and friends, who appreciated that this was a project I couldn't completely share, thanks for understanding my need to allow women to be heard without being punished for revealing themselves.

When you enter a marriage, you open a door.
To leave, you must close a thousand.
—Gretchen Cryer, author of
I'm Getting My Act Together and Taking It on the Road

Secret Loves

Introduction

This is a book about love and self-fulfillment and finding a life worth living. It is a book about courage and risk, but it is also about mother love and loyalty to the commitment that is marriage. It is a book about women whose true selves have been emotionally or sexually buried alive in marriages that are boring or loveless or worse, but who find a secret escape hatch in the form of long-term lovers who breathe life back into them, give their existence meaning once again, and instill in them a sense of joy and comfort and the will to go on.

But let me be perfectly honest with you. I didn't know all that when I began this project more than two years ago. I knew that I was on to a fascinating phenomenon, but at the beginning the idea of women with double love lives seemed simply deliciously intriguing. I was curious, and I was certain other people would be curious as well. I wondered why these women chose this life-style. I wondered how they truly felt, as wives and mothers, about what they were doing. And I certainly wondered how on earth they orchestrated such a complex life, given the fact that most of us have enough trouble coping with one marriage plus children and a job. I wanted to know how women with second, de facto, marriages, often lasting for decades, found the time and energy to handle two relationships.

I learned the answers to those questions—but I learned a great deal more. I learned that the women's issues we have all been dealing with in the thirty-odd years since the rebirth of American feminism are still far from being solved. In spite of all the hue and cry about the need for egalitarian relationships between men and women, many wives are still being swallowed up in the institution of marriage. Yes, there has been a surge of women in the work force over the last few decades, but women are still doing the majority of the work at home and still being cowed in private by men who rule the roost in one way or another.

The women in this book have found an ingenious solution to the problem. Each woman, without destroying her marriage or disrupting the lives of her children, has formed a relationship with a lover who is everything her husband is not. The resulting tandem life-style—married with lover—answers the question Erica Jong posed in *Fear of Flying* when she had her adulterous heroine say: "I felt properly appreciated for the first time. Do two men perhaps add up to one whole person?"

I feel privileged to have met the women whom I interviewed for this book, and privileged that they trusted me enough to put their lives in my hands. What I'm particularly proud of is that this is not so much a book *about* women as it is a book *by* women. These are real voices, real lives, not the stuff of fiction. This book is not conjecture. It is the way things really are. Yes, certainly, as a psychologist I have drawn some professional conclusions about the behavior of the women I interviewed, and I have also looked long and hard at what their stories mean, given the social climate in which we live. Yet I could not have done my work without the unselfish, totally candid contribution of the women themselves.

They were shy at first, many of them, afraid to reveal the secrets they had kept for so long. But once they began to speak, once they began to feel that they were talking to me woman-to-woman, there was a great rush of words, a torrent of feelings that had been buried for a lifetime. Many of the wives expressed immense relief that this story, as a compendium, was being told at last.

One woman said: "I always figured I wasn't the only one doing this. Now you're telling me there are a lot of us. All I hope is that by opening up to you, I'm making my little contribution to the world. What I mean is that I hope somebody, even just one person, will read my story and learn a lesson and not get trapped in a marriage the way I did. That would make me feel so good, to know that I helped somebody. We all have only one life to live. Women have to understand that you won't live that life well if you are not in a position to call the shots about your life. But if you ask me, most wives are not in a position to call the shots. I sure hope my daughter figures that one out. I've tried to teach her, but of course, I can't bad-mouth her father and I can't tell her the truth about my lover. Wait a minute! Maybe *she'll* be the person who reads this, and she won't know it's me, but she'll finally learn something from her old mom!"

Maybe so. I know I learned something from this woman and from all the women who let me into their lives. The bad news is that there is still a great deal of sadness and subjugation and squandering of human potential in women's lives. But the good news is that for many women, the human spirit is indomitable. Even as these women are fiercely determined to preserve their marriages and protect their children, they can last only so long in an atmosphere that is not conducive to their own growth and pleasure. But when they have reached the point where they can't stand the strictures any longer, they don't burst the bonds altogether. They simply slip away, Houdini fashion, leaving a caricature of themselves in the marriage relationship while they find true fulfillment in the arms and heart of another love.

In many ways this book grew into a project beyond my early expectations. The original premise and structure had to be retooled as the truth of women's lives emerged during the interviews. The process was endlessly fascinating, and the final product is a much richer tapestry than I had anticipated it would be.

Here, then, for you to share, is the compelling story of women who find that they must betray their husbands in order not to betray themselves . . .

SF
February 1993

1

When Love Strikes Twice

The psychology of adultery has been falsified by conventional morals, which assume, in monogamous countries, that attraction to one person cannot coexist with a serious affection for another. Everybody knows that this is untrue.

—Bertrand Russell

As a clinical psychologist who has the good fortune not only to maintain a private practice but also to suggest answers to people's problems by writing columns and books and hosting call-in radio and TV shows, I thought I had heard just about everything. But the call that came in to my radio show in Detroit one day caught me off guard. The woman on the line was describing her twenty-year love affair with a friend of the family, a married man whom her husband and children knew well.

"I'm a good person," she said. "I belong to the women's club at my church, and I volunteer at the hospital. When my children were little, I did everything—den mother, class mother, car pools, the whole thing. I'm a good wife, too, I think. I cook and clean. My husband and I sleep together. He's never had any complaints. But this relationship I have with my lover is what changed my life from black and white to color—

you know, like that wonderful moment in *The Wizard of Oz*. The first time we made love, I seriously almost passed out from the pleasure. Once you've known something like that, how can you ever give it up? And it's not just the sex. My lover is also my best friend in the entire world."

I quickly realized that this woman was sharing her life—or more to the point, her lives—not simply to titillate. She wasn't toying with her men, and she didn't sound like a frivolous person. She said she really needed both these men, both these lives.

Listening to my radio show caller, I began to wonder whether she was simply a fluke or the first of her number to speak out. I don't mean that female adultery per se is a new story. Everybody knows by now that statistics from Kinsey and *Redbook* and *Ladies' Home Journal* and plenty of other surveys and polls concur that at least one-third of Americans of both genders indulge in extramarital affairs. Yet the very word *affair* is rife with connotations of just philandering, fooling around, having a fling, a dalliance, a tryst. For that matter, Linda Wolfe entitled her 1975 book on women and extramarital sex *Playing Around*. And she stated categorically: "Very few women I spoke with had *long-term affairs* [italics mine]. It was much more usual for me to meet women who had short affairs with men they saw only occasionally or sporadically for a year or two."

Yet almost two decades have passed since Wolfe wrote that passage—precisely the length of time my radio show caller had been leading a double love life. Had something changed in the interim? I was immensely intrigued with that possibility, both as a psychologist and as a woman, and I decided to do some research on the subject. I wanted to find out whether married women who felt unfulfilled in their marriages might be secretly proceeding to solve the problem in a way long thought to be a preserve of men. One of the most recent books to deal with the topic of female adultery, Dalma Heyn's *The Erotic Silence of the American Wife*, does include a reference to older women who have maintained long-term affairs. But Ms. Heyn's research and hypothesis were largely aimed at examining her subjects' sexual experiences and their struggle to come to terms with whether they were "good" or "bad." This was indeed an interesting way to approach the subject, but I suspected that there might be several other strata that had yet to be mined.

Looking further, I had no trouble finding references to female adultery in both fact and fiction, from anthropological conjecture about prehistoric times to scientific data concerning the present. Yet no-where—not even in the massive thirteen-volume work *The Mythology of All Races*—did I find *significant* references to wives with long-term lovers. Wendy Thomas, the reference librarian at Radcliffe's Schles-inger Library, which is dedicated to the preservation and dissemination of women's history, made a special effort to help me but at last con-cluded that this slice of the subject of female adultery either has been the best-kept secret in the world or is simply not widespread enough to have been worth reporting in depth. I found myself thinking, Not until now, that is. I had become convinced that long-term double love lives might be surprisingly common for married women at this point in our social history.

After all, in the thirty years since the publication of *The Feminine Mystique*—Betty Friedan's clarion call which reawakened American feminism—women in this country have come to believe that they deserve to have full, rich lives and that for some, the roles of wife and mother might not have the emotional soul satisfaction they yearn for. That being so, I reasoned that a great many of the women who were already entrenched in traditional marriages during the late sixties and early seventies, when the message of "women's lib" reached them, must have felt painfully ambivalent. They were surely inspired by the atmo-sphere of "consciousness raising," and yet I suspected that many of them couldn't justify disturbing the status quo in their families simply to follow newly kindled personal aspirations for relationships that might be more egalitarian or lusty than the ones they had formed as young women programmed to be happy housewives.

To be honest, I believe they must also have been afraid to shear themselves loose from their moorings. If a traditional, male-dominant marriage was an impediment to a woman's growth, it was also a safe place where she could appear competent without having to face financial responsibilities—or, for that matter, loneliness. I began to wonder whether a fair portion of wives—most of them boomers caught between the "Leave It to Beaver" legacy of the fifties and the have-it-all credo of the seventies—might not have found a solution in the form of a two-track existence that allowed them to preserve their "old" marriages while simultaneously experiencing a "new" (and better?) relationship as well.

But I put the idea on the back burner for a while as I pursued my own busy life as a working wife and mother. Still, I couldn't get the subject out of my mind. Then, one day, while in Los Angeles hosting my CNN TV show, "Sonya Live!" I had lunch with a dear friend. Out of the blue, she confided that she was involved in an affair that had lasted twenty-two years and that her husband still had no idea that she had ever been involved with anyone else.

The woman who had called my radio show popped into my mind. If there were two stories, surely there were many more. My curiosity was piqued. I urged my friend to give me the details of her life with two men. She launched into her story, and as she talked, the details of what my radio show caller several years before had said came back to me with absolute clarity. I realized with a jolt that what my friend had to say about the logistics and emotions involved in her secret life echoed precisely what I had heard from that anonymous woman. First of all, each woman emphasized over and over that her marriage was treated respectfully as her primary relationship. In the same vein, the women said that their lovers, both of whom were married, saw their own marriages as the primary relationship. Consequently, the clandestine couples practiced the utmost discretion, and they had in fact developed a set of "rules" so that they would never lose sight of what part the long-term affairs played in their lives. The goal was that the affairs would never become known to their husbands or their children. The couples were elaborately discreet, making absolutely sure that their marriages took precedence over the long-term affairs. My friend—let's call her Irene—gave me the specifics.

"You don't degrade your family or his, and family comes first. I make sure he gets his wife an anniversary present. I make sure that if she needs him, he goes home. I don't know his wife, and I don't want to know his wife. In fact, once he wanted to show me some vacation pictures, with the two of them standing there like Mr. and Mrs. Happily Married, and I couldn't look at them. I told him to put the pictures away. I did that out of respect for her. And I would never show him pictures of my husband.

"As for the way we orchestrate this, we meet every Monday and Thursday, when we are each supposedly taking clients out to dinner. We've done this for twenty-two years. The exceptions, of course, are when family birthdays or anniversaries fall on a Monday or Thursday or when a family member is ill or upset. Then we don't meet each other. It's that clear-cut and that simple. We have an understanding."

In other words, preserving the marriages is a paramount concern. In fact, both Irene and the radio show caller said pointedly that the affair was not a destructive force in their marriages and certainly not an act of revenge against philandering husbands—a motive commonly thought to be the impetus for much of female adultery. Rather, the affairs were paradoxically the very saving grace of their marriages, filling voids the wives believed would have become intolerable as the anniversaries went by had they not found emotional sustenance in the extramarital liaisons.

Beyond that, each woman stressed that sexual relations with the lover had not begun immediately. The radio show caller, whose lover was a friend of the family, had said she was emotionally involved with the man for five years before sleeping with him for the first time. As for Irene, she met her lover at work and "dated" him for two years before they became sexually intimate. Both women said they had given the sexual side of their affairs a great deal of thought, a fact which flies in the face of the popular sentiment that a person who has an affair is swept away and hops into bed against her better judgment. Certainly, there are people who react that way, and there are people who have serial affairs. However, while the radio show caller and my friend Irene were intensely attracted to and aroused by their lovers, they both had developed profound emotional relationships *before* giving in to sexual desire. And after that they were sexually faithful to their lovers, except that they also continued to sleep with their husbands, albeit often out of a sense of duty. They succeeded in compartmentalizing their sexual activity, an ability which has typically been ascribed only to men. In other words, the women managed to invest each relationship separately with genuine commitment and with sexual exclusivity, while professing an abiding fidelity to both relationships.

In addition, these women talked about how important friendship was in their second relationships. They conveyed a sense of parity and sharing, an enviably egalitarian spirit—which, by the way, both women said was missing in their marriages. In fact, they both said that while they felt little or no guilt about the extramarital sex, they did feel guilty about the *emotional* intimacy with the lovers. However, the guilt was not strong enough to make them change their behavior because the need for the affair was so strong.

Hearing that was what sent me into action. I wanted to find other wives with long-term lovers and find out why they felt they needed this life-style. First, I tested the waters by placing ads in local newspapers around the country for potential interviewees, and I also simply started asking people if they knew anyone who might confidentially share her story. I can honestly tell you that after that, whenever I was at a gathering of at least four women, one or more had a story to tell or a friend she knew who was leading a double life and might agree to talk with me. In short order I had scores of interviewees, and more responses kept pouring in, showing me just how widespread the "married with long-term lover" phenomenon is. That being so, I was eager to know whether the commonalities between the radio show caller's experience and Irene's experience represented a kind of across-the-board theme for the majority of women in similar life-styles.

The answer is a resounding yes. That is, all the women I interviewed wanted to preserve their marriages, and in fact, more than two-thirds have succeeded as of this writing. A few of those wives have—with much pain and reluctance—given up their lovers out of fear of disclosure. In other words, when push comes to shove, the women choose husbands over lovers, even if the latter meet more of their psychosexual needs. They give up the lovers with deep regret, but their loyalty to their husbands and their desire to protect their children outweigh their personal needs.

Even so, one-third of my sample did eventually get divorced. Still, this is a remarkably low number in light of the fact that the divorce rate for the general population stands at 55 percent and appears to be rising. Also, of those who got divorced, the vast majority belonged to a group of women in my sample who had discovered at mid-life a sexual orientation that led them to form long-term liaisons with female lovers. Put another way, just over two-thirds of my interviewees were wives with male lovers, and, of this group, a full 87 percent stayed married. As for the women with female lovers, they were in the main living with the female lover, and they said that the unexpected discovery of their newly evolved sexual orientation was so overwhelming they eventually had to leave their husbands. They did, however, agonize over leaving. Like all the women leading the married-with-lover life-style, they had struggled as long as possible to preserve their marriages, and they felt pain and ambivalence over their final choice. Not one of the women I spoke with was flippant or smug about her long-term affair, and over and over I heard the same sentiment: "I can't believe I'm living this way. Twenty years ago on my wedding day, if you had told me I would have an affair, and that it would go on for years, I would have told you you were crazy!"

And so, like the two women who first told me about their secret lives, all of the women with secret lives began their affairs with every intention of staying married—and most of them did. Whether they were full-time homemakers or working mothers and whether they were from big cities, small towns or rural areas, they all demonstrated incredible ingenuity in organizing a two-track life so that they were never discovered.

Also, like Irene and the radio show caller, the women I eventually interviewed told me that they had not begun the sexual aspect of their affairs until months, if not years, into the emotional relationship. Even those women for whom the affairs' salient satisfaction is sexual pleasure had established a friendship before going to bed with their lovers. This is not to say that the lovemaking isn't important. Indeed, even the women who said that their lovers' companionship is more important than sex did agree that sex with the lover is far better than sex with the husband. In fact, the women with female lovers have been the most emphatic in this regard, and one of them said to me, "I'm surprised you didn't hear my first orgasm with her. It was an explosion!"

Interestingly, however, all but a few of the wives have continued to sleep with their husbands throughout their affairs. Of the women who have not, one has a husband who is HIV-positive, two have husbands who have taken male lovers, and several have husbands who have simply lost interest in sex. A few others have husbands who have become impotent because of complications of diabetes or because of the side effects of medication to control high blood pressure.

As for the women who are still sleeping with their husbands, some continue to enjoy sex with their husbands, but many say they "just do it." They don't really feel anything, but they don't see this as a catastrophe, or as detrimental to their mental health, or in any way as a negative or difficult experience. One wife said: "I'm his wife, so we have sex. The emotional part has gone out of it for me, but that's okay. It's like setting the table or doing the laundry. You don't have to like it or get all excited about it. It's part of being his wife. And he has never noticed that I'm not really 'there,' so it's fine."

There is also a sense among many of the women that their husbands suspect that there is a lover in the picture but that the husbands don't say anything because they are privately relieved. These are husbands with low sex drives, and they are embarrassed not to fit the macho stereotype of the sexually voracious male. Consequently, they tacitly endorse their wives' extramarital liaisons, feeling thankful that someone else is meeting the needs they don't really want to fill. One wife told me that her husband actually suggested early in the marriage that she should have an affair. Initially she was deeply hurt by this, but as the years went by, their sporadic and dispassionate marital sex life left her more and more dissatisfied. At mid-life she met a man who became her "spark." He jump-started her sexual batteries, and she knew she could never deny herself again. She actually tried to tell her husband, but he just smiled and changed the subject, and they have continued with this unspoken agreement to this day.

Actually, this concept of a "spark," a man or woman who ignites the wife's sexual fires for the first time, is remarkably prevalent among the women I interviewed. Certainly, those wives who said that sex with their lovers is the most significant part of the relationships feel that they had never known the full extent of their sexual capabilities until sleeping with the lovers. But even wives who cite factors such as companionship and mutual regard as being the most important elements of their affairs did say that sex with their lovers had awakened aspects of their sexual nature which had lain dormant with their husbands.

A few report that they have been able to bring this newly burning physical passion back into their marriages, but most said it was unique to their lovemaking with the other men or women. And only a handful of the wives have been moved to experience their awakened sexual prowess with anyone other than the long-term lovers. As one woman put it, "My relationship with Danny is just as committed as my relationship to my husband. I would never cheat on him in a million years. He says he feels the same way, absolutely. He sleeps with his wife, and he sleeps with me. Period. I sleep with my husband, and I sleep with Danny. Period. Please don't think of me as promiscuous. I don't sleep around. I am a very good person, a moral person. I didn't ever imagine that I would have two men in my life, but that's what has happened, and I am one hundred percent faithful to them."

There were, however, some women in my sample who did have a number of brief, shallow affairs before they connected with the persons who became their lifelong lovers. These encounters were by and large frightening and overwhelming in that the wives felt out of control, driven to behave in a way which they themselves did not condone. And they were not satisfied by the affairs. Even so, the fact that they succumbed in spite of themselves underscores for me the intensity of their needs to fill the empty areas in their relationships with their husbands.

Actually, for many of the wives the emptiness was not so much physical as emotional. Like the first two women I spoke with, Irene and the radio show caller, scores of women talked about a glorious sense of connection with their lovers, a feeling of being best friends, of communicating without strain, of sharing and bolstering and being boon companions. "Jim and I have the proverbial mutual admiration society," said one woman of her lover. "We're soul mates. This is the most wonderful feeling. I feel good about myself, validated, for the first time. I remember that before I met Jim, I sometimes used to ask myself why I was born. I wasn't suicidal or anything, but I just didn't see anything special about myself. And my husband certainly doesn't make me feel special. He just puts me down all the time. He's not a bad guy, but he makes remarks, criticizes me, belittles me. I guess he has to build himself up by cutting me down or something. But now I don't even care. Jim has given me my sense of self-worth. I have no intention of leaving my husband, but I would not give up Jim for anything. Are you kidding? He's the whole reason I feel like getting up in the morning. And you know something? This may just be a coincidence, but I've been a much healthier person since I started my relationship with Jim. I used to get colds all the time, have allergies, stuff like that. Nothing really serious, just nuisance ailments. But now I almost never get sick. And my blood pressure and cholesterol level have gone down. I'm not kidding. I feel great. I feel *younger* even!"

In fact, this woman's improved health and general sense of vigor and well-being probably are a direct result of her long-term affair. For one thing, it has long been known that people who feel beloved are not as prone to heart attacks as are people who feel abandoned or live alone. According to James J. Lynch, Ph.D., the author of *The Broken Heart: The*

Medical Consequences of Loneliness and *The Language of the Heart: The Body's Response to Human Dialogue,* the phrase *broken heart* is not just a metaphor. He reports that the rate of death from heart disease for people under the age of seventy who are not in loving relationships is ten times greater than for others. Lynch, who is director of the Life Care Health Institute in Towson, Maryland, also states unequivocally that touch has definite positive effects on cardiovascular health. His studies show that a loving touch can cause a dramatic lowering of heart rate and blood pressure and that lack of physical contact can have devastating effects on the cardiovascular system.

In addition, several recent studies have shown that close relationships have a direct, if still mysterious, effect on the immune system. Dr. Janice Kiecolt-Glaser, a psychologist at Ohio State University Medical School, completed an elaborate study which revealed that marital discord seriously weakens the immune systems of the couples involved.

And Dr. Sheldon Cohen, a psychologist at Carnegie Mellon University, along with Dr. Jay Kaplan, a psychiatrist at Bowman Gray School of Medicine in Winston-Salem, North Carolina, writing in the September 1992 issue of the journal *Psychological Science,* conclude that "affiliation protects animals from the potentially pathogenic influence of chronic stress." Cohen and Kaplan did a longitudinal (or long-range) study of macaque monkeys, subjecting one group to constant shifting of cage companions while allowing a control group to remain in closely bonded relationships. The latter showed great affection for one another, snuggling close and grooming each other, while the monkeys who were moved from group to group spent all their time establishing dominance and fighting. At the end of the trial the monkeys with no close relationships turned out to have seriously weakened immune systems, while the others were remarkably healthy. The scientists inferred that the same would be true for humans, who are, after all, social animals. Dr. Cohen specifically believes that what helps most is a firm belief that the people close to you are on your side and will help you if you need them. He says simply that "your relationships need to match your needs."

Obviously, the wives with long-term lovers in my study did not feel that their relationships with their husbands matched their needs. The instinct for self-preservation is strong, and so the wives in essentially unhealthy relationships sought healthier ones. This answers my crucial question of *why* wives—nice, ordinary, decent, often God-fearing wives—would feel a need for a secret life with a lover. The wives are desperate, for one thing, to find genuine sexual pleasure. But they are also seeking to be noticed and listened to with respect. They want, in a word, friendship. For whatever reason, their marriages do not fill all—or in some cases *any*—of these needs, and yet the wives remain fiercely committed to preserving the status quo even as they reach outside for psychological nourishment and physical satisfaction.

This demonstrates a verity I had long suspected: Women with little power in this society—plus the risk of enormous negative sanctions should they overtly break the rules—show a great deal of inventiveness in meeting their inner needs. Many of the wives with long-term lovers are responding to the strictures of our culture, which in practice continues to thwart and squander women's potentials, often leading them to make hasty commitments early in life even as it pays lip service to the ideal of equality of the sexes. For example, a large number of the wives I spoke with said that they got married as young women because they were "in love." Yet on closer examination I saw clearly that there is far from a single definition of what being "in love" means. In fact, I think we need to recognize that at this point in our society saying that one is marrying for love is simply the only acceptable response. Who would risk being called a gold digger by announcing that she was marrying up? Or that she wanted a man to take care of her because she was afraid to strike out on her own in a world that still pays women subsistence wages and that only within recent memory began to allow females such privileges as homeownership and credit lines? Who would admit, even if she could analyze herself clearly, that she was marrying to escape a bad home situation?

Actually, I was very taken with the fact that some form of dysfunction in their families of origin caused many of the wives to feel the need for two men. The women in the study, in the main, did not come from self-described happy homes in which parents loved each other and loved their children. Yet for the majority of these women, seeking a two-track love life should not be viewed as a pathological response but as a response to a pathological situation. Frankly, it's hard not to admire their optimism. These brave survivors who had no childhood models of what it means to be a family, and no personal experience with how people should treat one another, refused to give up on the possibility of finding a happy relationship. Their homes were battlegrounds, with an unhealthy cast of characters that might have included a jealous mother who resented the father's affection for the daughter . . . a father who left or emotionally abandoned the children . . . parents who were philanderers . . . parents who neglected the children . . . parents who emotionally and/or physically abused each other and the children. These childhood homes were devoid of warmth, affection, care, and, in many cases, simple respect. Is it any wonder that women coming out of such homes would have trouble making a good choice of a mate, especially since most of them rushed into the arms of the first "saviors" who agreed to marry them and thus rescue them from the hell of their parents' homes? And is it a surprise that women who grew up watching wives treated disrespectfully have no clear idea of what they deserve, or that boys growing up in such homes know only that it is acceptable to treat women badly?

What *is* amazing is that while these women frequently make a poor choice of a first mate—often unerringly heading straight for men just like their critical or emotionally unavailable fathers—they do have somewhere deep inside them an innate sense of what they need in order to be affirmed. Then, after they have grown and matured over the years in their marriages, they meet a person who can offer them for the first time in their lives a healthy intimacy. They love and they are loved, and they blossom. And yet by this time they are so firmly entrenched in their marriages and families and life-styles that they cannot bring themselves to destroy everything. Thus, the secret loves begin—and are sustained, in many cases, for the rest of their lives.

The wives who revealed all this to me do not represent a perfect random sample or a nationwide survey. I simply wanted the real voices of real women. One hundred and thirteen of them made up the final tally. They are from various ethnic and racial backgrounds—Caucasian, Asian, African-American, Hispanic, and mixed race. They are from all socioeconomic strata. There are Ph.D.'s and physicians, lawyers and farm wives, teachers, social workers, hairdressers, real estate saleswomen, full-time housewives, military women, women in publishing and entertainment—some of them very well known in their fields. Some are extremely wealthy, and others are barely making it.

They range in age from twenty-three to seventy-six, with the bulk of them at mid-life, but with a fairly even distribution overall. This makes abundantly clear the fact that women of *any* age are interested in sex, in relationships, in being affirmed, in wanting to give and receive love and affection, and particularly in having a sense of being meaningfully connected to another person.

The women are scattered all over the country: Oregon, Georgia, California, Colorado, Florida, Pennsylvania, Connecticut, New York, Michigan, Ohio, Missouri, South Carolina, North Carolina, Minnesota, Kentucky, and Maine. There are war brides, wives from England, Trinidad, and Jamaica. They all responded to my questionnaire and subsequently gave me long, heartfelt interviews. This is not to say that the women jumped at the chance to gush about their alternative way of living. In fact, most of them were reticent at first, torn between wanting to share their souls and needing to continue to keep the secret they had meticulously guarded for so long. However, I am grateful that I was able to gain their trust, assuring them of confidentiality and anonymity, agreeing to change all names and enough details so as not to wreak havoc with their lives.

Listen for a moment to these voices of just four of the many women who have let me—and now you—into their secret lives.

❧**Laura's story:** "I can't live without him. I don't know what to tell you. We fit together like two halves of a jagged puzzle—like those cantaloupes carved in fancy restaurants. All the things that are missing in my marriage, Hugh gives me. See, I married George, and worked as a secretary to put him through law school, because my mother thought that marrying a professional man was the be-all and the end-all. So I'm her pride and joy. And I'm miserable. I'm married to George—and he's married to his career.

"Then I met Hugh, in my creative writing class. We were in the same study group, and he would fill in my words, finish my sentences. We were soul mates from the start. So what was I supposed to do? I had three kids by then. I'm a nice Italian girl. Was I going to break up a family, tell my kids I didn't love Daddy anymore? Then again, was I supposed to give up Hugh, the man who makes me feel like someone worthwhile for the first time in my entire life? Believe me, sex is just a small part of this. In fact, if I feel guilty at all about my relationship with Hugh, it's because of the emotional closeness, not the physical aspect..."

═══════

❧**Myra's story:** "Marriage isn't where I really saw myself. Not a suburban housewife/mommy marriage anyway. From the time I was a little kid from the Bronx I saw myself as, say, the chairman of Twentieth Century-Fox. Seriously! But by the time I was twenty-something, with a secretarial school diploma and a drudge job as a receptionist in a second-rate video production company, reality began to set in. Then I met Eddie. He was smart and funny, and he had an Ivy League education and rich parents. He wanted to be the chairman of Twentieth Century-Fox, too. So we teamed up. I know now that I was trying to fulfill my ambitions through a man. Eddie was going to take me straight to the top. Well, we moved out to L.A., and we put together the best little TV production house in the West. We were the perfect team. He was the bread, and I was the filling, real smooth like a turkey melt. I always let him have the opening remarks. I knew a man made a more powerful impression. And he knew I was the one with the ideas—but we never let anyone else know. Still, it's hard to have a terrific personal life with your business partner. Especially after a while. He started getting jealous of my brains and talent, and I started resenting him for getting most of the credit for my stuff.

"Maybe that's why I let Jimmy into my life. He's young and gorgeous, and what we have is strictly sexual. Well, that's not quite true. He probably lusts after my power, which is a nice switch. Actually, I could have had my pick of young guys trying to get a start in the business. But Jimmy is perfect, and we've been together now for almost five years. A part of me would shrivel up and disappear without him at this point. But divorcing Eddie would upset the applecart, destroy our image, our business, our circle of friends. I just can't see doing that . . ."

⸻

◗**Kitty's story:** "There's nothing like being married to a CPA. You have to keep everything in order, save every grocery receipt. God forbid you should move an ashtray. What ever happened to the fun-loving civil rights activist I fell in love with in the sixties? He sure did a disappearing act! True, Carl is the father of my two beautiful children, and he makes a good living. We have a lovely home in Westport, Connecticut. I know I shouldn't complain. But this wasn't how I thought it was going to be. It's like we're cutouts, two-dimensional paper dolls. And he sees me as a possession. Really. He told me I had to take up golf because I had gotten too fat after the last baby. Fine! I didn't like being fat either, but I also didn't like being ordered around. Anyway, he hired a golf pro for me. And Susanne has turned out to be the best thing that ever happened to me. She's been my lover for six years now. She really cares about me, in a profound way that Carl couldn't even fathom. I have no intention of giving up this part of my life, ever . . ."

❧Ginger's story: "The annual pool party for Chet's office staff had gone beautifully, if I do say so myself. Chet agreed. He put his arm around my waist, and we watched the sunset as the last of the guests were leaving.

" 'You are the best wife and the best hostess in the world,' he whispered in my ear, and then he kissed me on the cheek. I looked out on our three acres of wooded property, our Olympic-size pool, our beautiful garden. Behind us was our home, a five-bedroom contemporary. But best of all, still splashing in the pool were our two beautiful children. Not only that, but ten-year-old Danny and eight-year-old Kate were being watched as always by dear Louisa, the Jamaican au pair who has been with the family ever since Chet and I were married eighteen years ago.

"Eighteen years. And I've still never had an orgasm with him. He's a white bread person. You know what I mean? He's not nourishing. He doesn't fill me up. He's a nice guy. My parents and everybody were so thrilled that I married well. But I feel nothing for him. Actually, that makes me really guilty since he's never done anything wrong, but feelings are feelings. You can't will yourself to love somebody.

"And the other way around. Ryan turns me on, in every way. He owns the health club I belong to. We've been together now for eight years. We just work it out. Like, right after that pool party, I told Chet I was going to a board meeting at the hospital, which started at seven. There actually was a meeting. We were trying to raise some more funds for the Child Life Committee. And I did go. But at about nine o'clock I excused myself. I drove to the health club, and Ryan was waiting, as we had arranged. We went into his office, which has a sofa bed, refrigerator, and microwave. This has always been our little hideaway. We started just as friends, but then after Kate was born, the relationship got sexual. It's indescribable. My orgasms are incredible. I still sleep with Chet, and I still don't have orgasms with him. Ryan still sleeps with Laura, his wife of twenty years. She's a bookkeeper for a fuel company and the mother of his three teenagers. He says their lovemaking can't compare to ours. But I always make him stop talking about that. I don't want to know.

"Anyway, sex is just a small part of this. In fact, the guilt I feel about my relationship with Ryan is because of the *emotional* closeness, not the sex. This is going to sound so corny, but Ryan feeds my soul. Chet's a nice guy, but to him I'm just the requisite wife to drape over his arm. I'm supposed to further his career and enhance his standing in the community. Even during our leisure time he calls the shots. I *hate* tennis, but I play doubles anyway. Part of the job description.

"Yet I do love Chet! I wouldn't hurt him—or the *children*—for the world. And I won't mince words. My husband has a very successful practice as an orthopedic surgeon, and I would be terrified to give up the security of the life I have with him. I married right out of college, and I've never been gainfully employed in my life except for baby-sitting as a teenager and waitressing a little. What would I do in the marketplace at this point? Just thinking about that makes my palms sweat. Even alimony and child support might not be enough to keep us going. You never know.

"So why do I risk my secret life with Ryan? Because I have to have a life worth living. Ryan gives me just that—the passion, the laughter, the tender little moments, the feeling that there's no one else like me, no one who could quite take my place—and, of course, the wonderful lovemaking. Maybe if I could meld my two men into one, I would. But I can't, so I guess I'll keep on needing them both, for different reasons. I didn't plan it this way, but I'll admit that living like this for so many years constitutes a conscious choice."

———

Do the stories of these four women shock you? I'll wager that the answer is no. In fact, I'll go so far as to suggest that what you felt as you read these revelations of "secret loves" was a gasp of recognition—either because you have always wondered what held some marriages together, or because you are the confidante of someone who has a secret life, or because you've felt the ache, the pull, of a possible second love and considered leading a dual existence yourself, or perhaps because you already have a sub-rosa relationship of your own. Certainly my intention in telling these stories was not to be judgmental. After all, life is not an on-off switch. Human nature being what it is, sex—and profound relationships—happen. Somewhere between rigid puritanical ethics and sex-crazed demons, real people fall in love, and make love, whether they're supposed to or not. True, in almost every culture since the beginning of time there have been religious and social laws and mores forbidding marital infidelity. And yes, the exceptions to this are far more likely to be the cultures or belief systems that allow men to have more than one woman—as in harems, mistresses, bigamy, polygamy—than the other way around.

But laws and mores have yet to prevent people from doing what they feel they must to survive—physically, emotionally, psychologically. In a very real sense the women who have opened up their secret lives to share their stories with you and me are doing just that. We're not talking here about casual encounters, one-night stands, fleeting affairs. Rather, the long-term-lover phenomenon is one in which women make a genuine commitment to two loves: a husband and a long-term companion, usually another man but sometimes a woman.

Yet all these women appear as ordinary as any of us. They are the woman next door, good mothers, grandmothers, and they are not at all careless about a two-track love life. They live an undercover but utterly serious life-style that involves a long—even a lifelong—simultaneous commitment to both a husband and a lover. And no one would ever know.

Still, even though I personally have set out to approach the subject in a nonjudgmental fashion, examining as objectively as possible this fascinating aspect of the repertoire of human behavior, there is no denying the fact that society punishes women who commit what amounts to adultery, whatever the motivation. This is why my subjects have been so careful to keep their lovers secret. Suzanne Frayser, an anthropologist at the University of Colorado who has studied infidelity in sixty-two societies from the ancient Hebrews to modern-day Eskimos, reports that there were no cases in which extramarital activity was permitted for women but not men, while the reverse was quite often true.

Of course, we don't have to look to ancient, remote, or primitive cultures to find strict ordinances and taboos against female adulterers. As short a time ago as 1989, twenty-eight-year-old Donna Carroll of Ashland, Wisconsin, faced two years in prison and fines of more than eleven thousand dollars, when her estranged husband, Robert, had his attorney dig up a vintage nineteenth-century law and subsequently had Donna arrested for adultery. (Robert had had a few paramours of his own, but he was not arrested.) Then, in 1990, Dawn Jakubowski of Norwich, Connecticut, was under arrest for adultery, a misdemeanor in that state punishable by up to a year in jail and a thousand-dollar fine, and two other Connecticut women were arrested shortly thereafter. One man was also arrested, but in these and other cases around the country involving a labyrinth of antiadultery laws still on the books in about half of the fifty states, the accused spouse is usually the wife. As Catherine Blinder of the Connecticut Commission on the Status of Women told *Time* magazine, "This is the 90s version of public flogging. Women have always been persecuted for infidelity" (*Time*, October 1, 1990). Indeed, in Brazil even today unfaithful wives are not merely persecuted but often killed with impunity by enraged husbands or even boyfriends. The courts accept a *legitima defensa de honra* (legitimate defense of honor), and in 1990, for example, in Belo Horizonte, with a population of 1.5 million, at least twenty-four allegedly unfaithful women were murdered by their husbands, with many more cases suspected.

Clearly, this and most other societies punish women for precisely the same activities and accomplishments for which men are rewarded: self-empowerment, sexual behavior, making money, getting into positions of power, the ability to be independent. The reason is not at all mysterious if we look at the big picture. Basically, society, in whatever form it has taken since before the dawn of recorded history, has been set up for the common good. Since the human female has a fairly long gestation period in order to produce most often one offspring at a time, and since the pregnancy is followed by months of nursing a virtually helpless newborn, women were simply not a good bet when it came to hunting woolly mammoths. As Scottish historian Reay Tannahill points out in her book *Sex in History,* "without food to sustain life, woman's ability to create it became irrelevant. At the peak of the Ice Ages it was man who kept the human race alive, and his social status at such times must have soared to gratifying heights." Tannahill goes on to remind us that at that moment in prehistory the male role in procreation was unknown, and humans had not yet developed "pair bonding," even though their presumed ancestors, a species of apes called gibbons, had done so. (Gibbons, by the way, are the only monogamous primates other than humans, probably because the female has a menstrual cycle, not an estrus cycle, and is thus available to her mate at all times for sexual activity.)

If man was superior during his home-from-the-hunt chapter in history, imagine what happened during the Neolithic era when he figured out how to domesticate livestock and subsequently inferred his own role in creating children. One ram, he must have at last realized, could impregnate, say, fifty ewes. As Tannahill wryly observes, "With power comparable to this, what could man not achieve?" On a personal level, of course, a male could now say "my son," and so he began to have a vested interest in saying "my wife." All previous marital customs—for example, polygyny (one man with many women) and polyandry (one woman with many men)—receded as, in Tannahill's words, "women's sexual activity began to be seriously curtailed." After that a man might be a bigamist or indeed support a harem if he could manage it, but like the gibbon, which has a special sound that means "Stay away from my wife," human males began to demand fidelity in monogamy from their wives in order to protect the concept—and the patriarchal bloodline— involved in the phrase *my son.* In fact, anthropologist Helen E. Fisher, from the American Museum of Natural History in New York and the author of *Anatomy of Love: The Natural History of Monogamy, Adultery, and Divorce,* told me that only 0.5 percent of all societies ever studied have permitted polyandry, and then only among the very rich.

In any case, as agriculture stabilized some male-dominant cultures, and nomadic pastoral societies underscored the position of women as chattel to a man, right along with the beasts he herded, we proceeded pell-mell into the Western Judeo-Christian culture that is our most recent heritage; which is to say that religious codes notwithstanding, a sexually adventurous man has traditionally been tolerated, or even secretly admired, while a woman has been enjoined to be chaste as a maiden and faithful as a wife. The motive for this was twofold: Men wanted to be sure they were the biological fathers of their wives' children, and they wanted to maintain the power inherent in an essentially master/slave relationship. True enough, the highly touted post-pill "sexual revolution" as well as the rebirth of feminism in the sixties and seventies went a long way toward loosening the strictures (or some would say, the morals) of this culture. In the most recent research that I came across, a survey of two thousand Americans conducted by James Patterson and Peter Kim and published as *The Day America Told the Truth,* almost one-third (31 percent) of both husbands and wives reported having affairs, and of these, 62 percent said they don't feel there is anything morally wrong with what they are doing. Beyond that, a majority of the women said they like their lovers better than their husbands. (The reverse was true for the men.) As Ken Doyle, a psychologist at the University of Milwaukee, reminds us, "Nathaniel Hawthorne's Hester Prynne got an A for Adultery. These days she'd probably only get a C."

Still, as the women in my sample are all too aware, even if an adulterous woman today escapes public shame or punishment, the penalty for getting caught is often swift and brutal in the form of the private tragedy of divorce. As women—particularly divorcées themselves—know all too well, the ever-increasing statistical frequency of the breakup of marriages in this country has not numbed the personal pain. Divorced women are largely accountable for what has been called the feminization of poverty, partly because of the difficulty of enforcing court-ordered child support payments and partly because women still earn far less on the average than do men, even in comparable jobs. Without a doubt, the prospect of being unable to live well herself, let alone being able to give her children a good life, is a chilling one for any woman.

In this arena we are frankly not so far from the Ice Age woman who needed the man to bring home the slain woolly mammoth. Call this feminist backlash all you want, but what I'm really saying is that women cannot, and should not have to, bring up the next generation alone. A great deal has been written about women's reentry into the workplace, about juggling, having it all, two-career couples, role-sharing marriages, even about single women choosing a sperm bank over a husband. Yet almost any pregnant woman, any nursing mother, any mother of very young children will tell you that being the partial support, let alone the sole support of the family during that period, is wrenchingly difficult.

And of course, there's no "right" time to be a single mother. School-age children, left to their own devices as latchkey kids, are incredibly vulnerable. Teenagers need supervision as well, given the current social milieu that fosters rampant drug and alcohol abuse among our youth, not to speak of sexual activity often beginning when youngsters have scarcely reached puberty. Also, children, whether they are toddlers or teens, need money put away for the future, for college and weddings and so on. Unfortunately, even if a divorced father does make good on his child support payments, the minute a youngster reaches the age of eighteen, the father is almost always legally off the hook and does not even have to help with his offspring's further education or medical expenses, let alone such "luxuries" as wedding plans. Given the fact that sixty thousand dollars is a conservative estimate of what a college education costs these days, and considering that even a modest wedding can cost thousands of dollars, divorced mothers are obviously hard pressed to provide single-handedly for their young adult children.

But even beyond these horrifying economic and social realities, I maintain that mothers know in their hearts that if a family is at all within the realm of functional, it is better off intact than rent asunder. I think of one friend of mine, freshly divorced after more than two decades of trying valiantly to make a troubled marriage work. "It's been rough," she said. "I couldn't keep up the mortgage payments, and my ex-husband wasn't sending any money, so I had to sell the house. I'll never forget the day we moved out of my kids' childhood home and into a little apartment. Just ordinary stuff made me cry: taking down the posters from the walls of their bedrooms, packing up the photo album with all the pictures of shared birthdays and Christmas mornings. So now we have a one-bedroom apartment. The kids have the bedroom, and I sleep on a sofa bed in the living room. We have a tiny table against one wall, with only three chairs around it. Oh, sure, we're going to be just fine, but you can't help feeling that there is something wrong with this picture."

With that poignant voice in mind, the fact that a woman in an even marginally acceptable marriage would risk everything by maintaining not just a fleeting affair but a full-fledged, long-term, outside liaison becomes even more breathtaking. She now has to bother about birth control with two men. She has opened herself up to another possible avenue to AIDS and other sexually transmitted diseases. And she simply has to summon the mental and physical energy necessary to cover her tracks constantly and elaborately. Oddly enough, as I have pointed out, the twist is that the women who do this are trying to *preserve* their marriages—and their own sanity. Over and over again the women I spoke with put a personal spin on the abiding sentiment that while their marriages in most cases appear to have everything that society affirms—money, security, two concerned parents—there is something clearly missing, whether it is a sense of fun or the experience of being seen as a desirable and intimate partner or simply the ability to reveal oneself and be vulnerable. Yet there are also intricate networks of emotional, financial, and social bonds holding husband and wife together.

Toni, now thirty-eight, is a perfect example. A good Catholic, she followed all the rules and met everyone's expectations by keeping a hope chest in high school, accepting an engagement ring from the boy next door upon graduation, working for a few years to save up for a house and baby, marrying at twenty-one in the gown her mother had picked out, and even slicing the cake her mother-in-law had chosen. After four miserable, almost sexless years, she tried to tell her mother that she had to get out of the marriage. "He doesn't drink, he doesn't beat you," her mother said. "Consider yourself lucky. Have children, be normal." Toni had been telling me her story with a bit of flair and wit until that point. Then she paused, made a kind of gasping sound, and inadvertently touched her throat. Her eyes widened. "I felt like I was dying," she told me in a small, choked voice.

But she didn't die—not psychologically, not sexually, not physically. Instead she took up with an older man, a family friend she had loved and admired even as a young girl. That was thirteen years ago. Charlie himself has a proper, passionless marriage and three children. Toni now has two cherished children of her own and is able to tolerate her marriage, although she confesses that since her husband makes a fine living and she doesn't work, she sees herself as a kept woman. "I've felt like a prostitute from the honeymoon on," she says. "But with Charlie, I feel honorable. You may think that is strange, but he is the most honorable man I have ever met. He makes me feel beloved and beautiful and bright and special. We laugh and cheer each other on. The sex is tender and yet passionate. I wouldn't destroy his marriage for anything in the world, and by now I can't imagine how I would begin to tear mine apart. So we'll just go on this way, being discreet, being happy at stolen moments when we can be together. Hey, no one has a totally happy life. I'll settle for the one I have. It's a lot better than unraveling the lives of everyone around us."

In one sense Toni is something of an anomaly since for all intents and purposes she had an arranged marriage of the kind that pretty much passed out of this culture in the nineteenth century. Far more of the women in my sample chose their own mates, many running away from intolerable home situations, hoping to escape by getting married. But the common denominator is the original and almost always impossible expectation that modern marriage will not just fulfill our economic and child-rearing needs but be a lifetime source of intimate companionship and sexual excitement. British sociologist Annette Lawson, whose study of infidelity is presented in her book *Adultery: An Analysis of Love and Betrayal,* points out that the intoxicatingly delicious and dangerous passions of romantic love, which once were the province of such thwarted young pairs as Shakespeare's Romeo and Juliet or of shameless sexual adventurers like Flaubert's Madame Bovary, somehow became the only acceptable basis for the institution of marriage itself. Not surprisingly, people are frequently disappointed as the routines of domesticity dim their ardor. Not only that, but as I have been made painfully aware in my private practice, too often people end up repeating the destructive marital life-styles of their own parents, even though they promised themselves they would never do so.

Then, too, the very institution of marriage itself begins to define people's roles and behavior. As the nineteenth-century author Samuel Rogers put it, "It doesn't much signify whom one marries, for one is sure to find next morning that it was someone else." In fact, in my clinical practice, I frequently see that for many people, the instant they become husband and wife—roles which they associate with their own parents—the specter of the incest taboo rears its head, making the couple feel as if they were going to bed with their parents. This problem, in fact, can pervade all aspects of the relationship, and often a man who was a happy-go-lucky and ardent suitor is transformed into a critical and domineering father figure to his wife. The situation can become dangerous to a woman's physical and mental health, as has been aptly demonstrated by the grande dame of American sociology Jessie Bernard, in her classic book *The Future of Marriage.* She shows that while traditionally men consider marriage a trap for themselves and a prize for their wives, statistically marriage is good for men—physically, socially, and psychologically. Conversely, Bernard makes it clear that while traditionally almost all women want to marry, statistically marriage actually makes legions of women sick.

Consider Charlotte Perkins Gilman, the maverick feminist whose writing during the early part of this century included a utopian novel called *Herland,* along with her most searing piece, a short story entitled "The Yellow Wallpaper." This powerful and finely crafted tale is largely autobiographical, written in the form of the journal of a well-married woman whose physician-husband insists that she take the then-famous "female rest cure" to help her stop pining to paint and write and adjust to her "natural roles" as homemaker and mother. The woman is taken to a country house for three months and confined to a sparsely furnished room. The walls are papered with an intricate pattern on a kind of moldy yellow color, and she stares at the paper day after day, growing more and more obsessed, fancying an acrid yellow smell hanging in the air and picturing a woman trapped behind the pattern, rattling bars to get out. In the end the heroine goes completely mad, claws the paper off the walls with her fingernails, and begins to creep incessantly along the baseboards of the room, until she is discovered by her husband, who faints dead away in shock. Gilman herself, in her first marriage, was subjected to the rest cure but managed to escape before she lost her mind. She wrote the story, she later said, to save other women from the perils of a marriage that made them either pampered pets or domestic slaves instead of full human beings.

And so the issues are multiple and complex. How does a woman, in a world that extols monogamy and fidelity, make a life that takes into account anthropologist Margaret Mead's famous assertion that there should be three marriages in a lifetime: "The first relationship is for sex; the second is for children; the third is for companionship"? Obviously some women, whether through luck or perseverance or a measure of both, manage this three-part scenario with one mate "until death do us part." A friend of mine tells me about a suburban woman, Nancy, the mother of four children ranging in age from eleven to eighteen and the wife of a successful engineer. Nancy and her husband have just celebrated their twentieth wedding anniversary, and Nancy maintains that she is sublimely happy and that her husband is "a saint who worships the ground I walk on." She says he loves the children, is involved in all their activities, and works hard but has time for recreation with her. He gives to the church and to charity. He has a sense of humor. And he's a wonderful lover. My friend, herself a divorcée, recalls being amazed when Nancy told her all this, and she congratulated Nancy for having made such a wise choice when so many women just rush into marriage without really knowing what they're getting into. "Oh, don't give me the credit," Nancy said. "I met him at a college mixer. He was really handsome, and I was flattered when he called the next day. We only dated a few months, and I hardly knew him at all when we got married. I'm just lucky, I guess."

Indeed, she is. But for others, as life spans lengthen and women continue to expand their options, the odds of finding one man who will provide all needs for all stages seriously diminishes. Some women today, whether by design or default, solve this problem with serial marriages. But as we have seen earlier, divorce is not a panacea by any means, even when remarriage is in the offing. In fact, according to data from the 1980 census, published in *American Women in Transition,* by Suzanne M. Bianchi and Daphne Spain, remarried couples are even more likely to divorce eventually than are couples in first marriages, partly because of the problems inherent in "reconstituted" or "blended" families.

I firmly believe that is why the women in this book have, consciously or unconsciously, chosen another path. They live two distinct "marriages" at the same time—usually a legal one that constitutes Margaret Mead's "child-rearing relationship," providing economic security, paternity for the children (whether or not the husband is their biological father), and standing in the community, plus a second, sub-rosa relationship that affords some combination of emotional openness and intimacy, romance, lovemaking, and companionship. Interestingly, given Mead's mention of one relationship for sex (usually early in adulthood) and another one (usually later in life) for companionship, the women in my sample tend to find that their lovers often fill the need for both sex and companionship, although one of these usually takes precedence over the other. In the meantime, the actual marriage, while showing no discernible signs of trouble, gradually becomes a façade.

The relationship often has no more depth than an eight-by-ten glossy in which Mom and Dad and the kids are captured smiling dutifully into the camera.

Some husbands are good fathers and adequate lovers but fall short when it comes to the friendship factor. In my sample the wives of men such as these are drawn to lovers who "appreciate" them, who talk until all hours of the night, who respect their interests or their talents, not just their physical attractiveness. Conversely, I spoke with other women who are married to good, steady providers who love and respect them and do good jobs of being a companion, but what goes on in bed is far from satisfying. If a wife in such a relationship has a healthy appetite for sex—either because she acquired a taste during the premarital years or married as a virgin and yearns to reach her full sexual potential—the likelihood of her succumbing to a passionate, enduring extramarital relationship is very great indeed.

But whether a woman is lured by a man who "understands" her, a man who sets her on fire, or another woman who offers the revelation of a previously unexplained part of her nature, the simultaneous commitment she makes to a husband and a lover is bound to create a heady emotional cocktail, not to mention a dizzyingly complicated day-to-day schedule that is not for the faint of heart. Just how this life-style works—or at times doesn't work—is what this book lays bare, in the sometimes heart-tugging, sometimes breathtaking words of the women themselves. Over brunch in Manhattan, lunch in Detroit, dinner in Los Angeles, in my own home, in their homes, in offices and coffee shops and malls, over the telephone, we talked like friends, freeing at last a long pent-up woman's story.

At the core what I have uncovered is a story about survival—about opening a window for ventilation in a marriage, rather than walking out the door and slamming it shut. It is about affirming one's self and feeling a greater sense of control. For many, it is about having a life worth living. Remember, these are women with a deep moral sense that they must maintain their marriages, and yet their marriages are not giving them what they need. There are often problems such as sexual incompatibility, or emotional abuse on the part of the husband, or simply a lack of parity and a feeling that the husband dominates the relationship so that the wife is not "allowed" to come into full bloom as a person. In other cases the wife manages to grow beyond her husband, in effect shedding old, constricting skin and emerging as a new and larger being. For other couples, the marriages have just simply worn out over the years. Often, in spite of a shared history, a husband and wife find that there is nothing much left between them, nothing more to say, no more dreams to dream, nothing in common anymore. Even more frequently, there was really nothing much to the relationship from the beginning, but the routines and responsibilities of domesticity kept the couple busy enough for a while, particularly when the children were young. Yet whatever the specifics of the scenario, the wife reacts by finding a new love, one who fulfills her and lets her be all she can be.

Actually, if you think about it, the entire history of humankind, in all its diversity, is just that: the determination to survive and thrive, not only physically but mentally, emotionally, spiritually. The women in this book who have let me—and now you—into their lives seem simply to represent another variation on a theme as old as human nature itself. I am neither condemning nor condoning their behavior, but by reporting it, I hope to offer greater insight into what women's lives are like and why some of them take a nontraditional path. For indeed, the women I met were fiercely determined to keep growing and evolving, and they were equally determined to keep their marriages and their families intact. With astonishing energy and planning, the vast majority of them succeeded.

What does the secret love phenomenon mean for the people involved and, more important, for the state of marriage and family life in this society? Are these women sinners, or are they doing the best they can to remain psychologically intact and at the same time keep all their loved ones, children included, from being hurt? Is it possible to have woven a fabric of life so tightly as a young woman that to rip everything apart would be a kind of emotional suicide and murder for everyone involved? Consider the fact that Judith Wallerstein's landmark study of the children of divorce left no doubt that the impact of a dissolved marriage is deep and indelible on all members of the family. We now know that the children of divorce have an even higher divorce rate than the general population.

This, I have learned, is why a secret love, for at least some women, is the lesser of two evils. The women I came to know who maintain outside loves do not see themselves as dishonest and immoral adulteresses, but as women who have found the best way they can to fulfill their basic needs for love and touch without destroying those around them. As one woman said to me, "If I am an adulteress, which man am I cheating—the husband I no longer love or sleep with, who never makes me feel desirable in any way . . . or my true friend and lover, with whom I've shared twenty magnificent years, the man who still makes my heart skip a beat and who makes me feel totally alive?"

2

I Want Some Body to Love

The lover in the husband may be lost.

—*Lord Lyttelton*

Katherine and I met for lunch in my New York apartment. The week before, when I telephoned to make the appointment, I had suggested a well-known East Side restaurant for our rendezvous, but she let out a horrified gasp.

"I grew up near there," she said in a hushed voice, even though she had already told me that she was alone in the kitchen of the Westchester County home she shares with David, her husband of nine years, and their ten-month-old son, Davey. "I went to Brearley," she continued, referring to an exclusive private girls' school. "I hung out in all the right places. People are still there who knew me then. What if someone was at the next table and overheard me telling you . . . everything."

"Everything," as it turned out, is a compelling, poignant, and searingly passionate story. The saga started when Katherine, now thirty-one, was twenty-five and had been married for three years, and it continues in all its fierce pain and exquisite pleasure to this day. Once she began to talk, the tale virtually told itself. Yet getting started wasn't easy for Katherine, a lithe blonde with cover girl good looks. Even in the privacy of my living room, she hesitated, shifting the pillows on my sofa, sipping a little tea, and staring out the window for a long time. I didn't push her. Then, unexpectedly, she looked me straight in the eye, as though she suddenly understood that she needed to say this, in strictest confidence, to someone who wouldn't judge her and wouldn't punish her—and might even offer the comfort of woman-to-woman empathy.

"I grew up assuming I would marry and have children, and I got married right on schedule, the week after I graduated from Radcliffe," she said. "David was the perfect match for me socially. He had graduated from Andover and Harvard and had just finished his first year of law school. I was going on to grad school to become a social worker, and we already had a nice little apartment in Cambridge. Both of us had family money to get us through school, and our wedding was right out of a fairy tale—a perfect June day on Martha's Vineyard, with all the trappings."

She paused for a moment as her eyes misted over and focused on a remembered scene that only she could see. "I'm quite religious actually," she said. "Standing in the sunshine in my wedding gown, looking at dear David, and saying those sacred vows, I was silently praying for the strength not to break them." Then she laughed. "After all, like a lot of women my age, I had been around. I had never been faithful to a boyfriend, that's for sure! Fidelity was a whole new concept for me. But I wanted to make it work."

As it happened, during the following three years, while David finished law school and started his practice in Scarsdale, a tony New York City bedroom community, Katherine had no problem "making it work."

"I flirted a little with the guys in my classes at BU," she said. "But I wasn't even tempted to do more than that. My marriage was fine, kind of low maintenance with both of us studying all the time and once in a while eating out or going to a concert or the movies or to visit our parents. The sex was okay, nothing spectacular, but nothing to complain about. I mean, I had orgasms, he had orgasms. So it wasn't earth-moving every time—so what? I was mature enough not to expect a peak experience every time we went to bed."

Then, after the move to Scarsdale, Katherine parlayed her brand-new master's degree in social work into a better-than-entry-level administrative spot in the Human Resources Administration for the New York City government. "I thrived on commuting to the city, which had been my first home after all," she said. "The suburban thing was OK, but it was more David's idea. Eventually I wanted to be a full-time mother, but I saw that as a phase, not a lifetime career. So I became a real dynamo at work, on the theory that I'd have a track record and be able to get back in after a child-rearing hiatus. I had my life planned—all of it."

All of it, that is, except for meeting Joey. "He got a job in my department a year after I did," Katherine said with a lilt to her speech that I hadn't heard before. "I saw him at the water cooler, and I just started some pleasant small talk like 'Aren't you new here?' He was kind of shy but obviously so thrilled to have the job and glad someone had taken the trouble to speak to him. I figured he was a couple of years younger than I am, which turned out to be true. Also, he comes from a working-class family, so he was somewhat in awe of me. For a long time I felt kind of motherly toward him, nothing more."

She couldn't suppress a slightly sly smile at that point. "Something happened. I can't even explain it. He's not really as handsome as my husband, not as tall, not as distinguished. But something happened. We had been getting friendlier and friendlier for close to two years. At the same time I was trying to get pregnant, and the sex at home had turned into a clockwork nightmare, with temperature taking and charts and a roller coaster of emotions every time my period was late and then it would come and we'd start over again. We were even talking about getting infertility tests, and I was feeling like a freak of nature, a barren woman. Never in my life had I imagined I would be anything but the Earth Mother, having natural childbirth and nursing and everything, but I couldn't even conceive!"

Katherine stood up at this juncture and paced from the sofa to the window and back before she went on. Her body language told me that all the frustrations and sense of failure of that period of her life had come back full force with the telling of it. "Oh, sure," she finally said, "David could have been the one who was infertile, but I couldn't believe that. I had to blame myself. So anyway, one day when Joey and I went for coffee, I blurted out the whole story. He was so supportive, so kind, and he reached across the table and touched my hand." She shivered even at the memory of that moment.

"Electric currents, shock waves," she said, grinning broadly. "I called home with an excuse about working late that night, and Joey and I went to a hotel. We used a condom, because I figured the irony would be that I'd finally get pregnant with the wrong man's child—and also because of AIDS, I guess. But the sex was practically supernatural. It was like a drug. I had never experienced anything like it before. I didn't know such feelings were even possible."

That was four years ago. Joey has since married a childhood sweetheart from his neighborhood in Brooklyn, and Katherine conceived at last and gave birth to a son, who, at almost a year, looks just like his father's baby pictures. As Mrs. David J. Wilson III, Katherine is a full-time homemaker, Junior League volunteer, and perfect hostess for her husband's clients. Her parents and her in-laws are immensely proud of her, calling her their "golden girl," particularly since her sister has yet to marry and her sister-in-law is already divorced. But Katherine still sees Joey.

"They'd all be shocked," she said. "The whole community would be shocked. And getting away with it, getting into the city, is a lot harder now. I spend a great deal of time fantasizing about Joey, pining for him. On the morning of a day when I know I'm finally going to see him, I'm shivery with anticipation. Then, when I'm with him, I feel almost unbearable excitement sexually—yet very safe and comfortable. It's as if there is no one else in the world. I've tried to break this off, but I can't stand to be without him. The passion is so strong that I give in and call him. It's like needing a fix. I have to have Joey."

While she was talking, I had been putting lunch on the table. We sat down and started with bowls of steaming split pea soup, laced with rosemary and thyme. Comfort food. At first we savored the soup in silence. And then I asked Katherine if she ever felt guilty.

"A little," she said. "But you know, I honestly think the affair has improved my marriage. For one thing, I'm a lot sexier with David after I've been with Joey. The effect can last for weeks. And besides that, my relationship with Joey makes me more tolerant of little things that might annoy me about David—just whether he leaves his dirty socks on the floor or shaving cream on the bathroom mirror. I'll be just about to blow up at him and then I'll think, Give the guy a break. You're cheating on him, after all!

"But if I don't really feel all that guilty, I have to admit that I feel a lot of fear—about getting found out, I mean. Until my son was born, I kind of took my marriage for granted. But the minute I knew I was pregnant, I felt so vulnerable. I've read about single mothers leaving their babies in day care and working full-time, and I just can't see how they manage. Emotionally, financially, how could you live like that?"

And yet she continues to put her marriage, and presumably Joey's marriage, in jeopardy. Katherine blushed. "I know it sounds crazy," she said. "I don't know whether David would leave me if he found out, but I think he'd give me a chance to break up with Joey. See, he had a brief affair once, during that awful period when we were trying to get pregnant. It was nothing, just a way to prove his masculinity, I think, and he told me about it. I was terribly hurt, but I got over it. So anyway, there's a precedent. David is an honorable man. And he wouldn't want to destroy our family. He'd want to end this thing quietly, and he'd probably never bring it up again. At least that's what I tell myself every time I get a baby-sitter and say I'm going into the city for a matinée, and he thinks I mean a Broadway show." She laughed nervously and toyed with her salad. I asked her then if she ever wished she were married to Joey. She put down her fork, looking genuinely startled.

"Never," she said, as though she had not once entertained that thought until I brought the subject up. "I probably wouldn't have married Joey even if I had met him first. What we have between us isn't the sort of thing that could survive day-to-day stuff, paying bills, taking out the garbage. Anyway, he'd be so uncomfortable around my family and friends. He jokes about the gardener making love to the debutante. But it just so happens that we can't keep our hands off each other."

———

After I walked Katherine to the elevator, I asked if she thought she'd go on having two men in her life. "Forever," she said without hesitation. "As long as David never finds out. I honestly love my husband, and he gives me companionship, security, intellectual stimulation. He's a wonderful father, and I'd like to have another child. But with Joey, everything is amplified, intense, and the sex is the kind that a man like David could never give me. So I have the best of both worlds. I could go on like this always."

Will she? Katherine is young, still thirty-something, and we have no way of knowing what her future holds. But if a great many of the other women in my sample are any indication, Katherine may well continue with her two-track love life for a lifetime, particularly because she falls into the subgroup of wives—one-fifth of my sample—whose lovers primarily fill sexual rather than emotional, companionship, or security needs. This is not to say that Katherine and women like her do not feel any sense of friendship with their lovers. Quite the contrary. Like Katherine, all these wives had developed close relationships with the men who became their lovers long before they first slept with them. And the sense of mutual admiration and caring remained an essential ingredient in the relationships. However, once the relationships became sexual, once the "spark" had ignited the flames of passion, that aspect became the primary force that gave reason to their relationships. There are, as we shall see in subsequent chapters, women for whom this is not so. That is to say, while all the wives with long-term lovers receive from their lovers some degree of companionship, sexual pleasure, and personal affirmation, the pulling power of each of these elements differs for each subgroup of women. What is interesting is that those women who found sexual pleasure to be the strongest aspect of their relationships with their lovers were the *least* likely even to fantasize about leaving their husbands, and in fact, not one of the wives in this group has ended her marriage, and all but a small fraction are still sleeping with their lovers as well. Virtually all these women echoed Katherine's assertion that leaving the marriage for the lover was unthinkable, but that ending the relationship with the lover was also out of the question.

Listening to woman after woman give her own version of this story, I came to understand that what has happened in these cases is that the women have thoroughly internalized the concept that someone who is a "good" wife and mother cannot also be a "bad girl" in bed. Such a woman is actually afraid to abandon herself to sexual pleasure with her husband because she is convinced, rightly or wrongly, that he will be shocked by her carnal nature and perhaps even leave her in search of a more "virtuous" mate. I was not surprised to find that the vast majority of the women who fell into this category had very strict religious backgrounds, as well as parents with extremely high expectations for their daughters in terms of behavior that would be "acceptable" within the families' ethnic, religious, or social milieus—that is, marrying the "right" man, being a solid citizen, and generally playing by the rules. In fact, I suspect that until recently such women simply denied their sexual natures and lived out their lives in proper but joyless unions.

The wives in my sample, however, by and large came of age when reasonably reliable birth control, on the one hand, and a social climate of sexual "permissiveness," on the other, combined to give women the option to explore the pleasures of their sexuality. That being so, one might think they would have shaken the idea that they can't/shouldn't be sexy in the marriage bed, but that is not what happened. Instead they have split themselves in a self-imposed version of the well-known Madonna/Whore syndrome—a variation which I call the Wife/Wench syndrome. In the former it is the husband who sets his wife on a pedestal and gets his "baser" needs met elsewhere. In the latter it is now the wife who defines herself as a "nice lady" in the marriage and then, as Kenny Rogers sings, "takes her love to town," where she lets loose her bawdy persona. This is not to say that the husbands are blameless. Many of them did have a Madonna/Whore attitude, one which only exacerbated the Wife/Wench women's own sense of needing to split themselves in two.

Yet why, I wondered, did these women form attachments with long-term lovers, rather than indulge in the sporadic affairs more common years ago? The answer, I believe, is that back then many women were engaging in what I call postmarital dating. Today, however, the majority of women go into marriage already sexually experienced. They don't need to experiment because they have previously played the field. Bearing this out, I found that the older women with whom I spoke, those who had married as virgins or who had "known" only their husbands, did in fact engage in some postmarital dating before settling into the relationships that became the long-term lover liaisons. Typically they went through a flurry of short, strictly sexual relationships. Just as typically these experiences not only were not satisfying but were frightening. One woman recalls waking up in a man's bed, after an evening of having had too much to drink and not even knowing where she was.

"I was horrified," she told me. "I had gone to the happy hour at a neighborhood bar when my husband was out of town on business and my kids were at summer camp. I'm not much of a drinker, and I had let this guy buy me one drink after another. Don't ask me what happened after that. I'm just not used to that much alcohol. So the whole thing terrified me. How could I have let everything get out of control like that? But see, looking back, I have to say that I wanted to sleep with someone besides my husband because I didn't want to go to my grave never having slept with anyone but him. I was a virgin when I got married in 1965. I was twenty years old. And sex with my husband wasn't anything like what I read about in magazines and novels. I never felt anything. He just rushed through it and rolled over and started snoring.

"So the years went by, and I started feeling so sad about that. We'd have sex, he'd fall asleep, and I would get up real quietly and go into the kitchen and smoke and look out at the night sky. Sometimes I'd cry, but I tried hard not to because I didn't want my eyes all puffy in the morning. If I did cry, I'd put ice under my eyes before I went to bed. Then I'd start laughing at myself, standing there at one in the morning in a robe, with a cigarette in one hand and a plastic bag of ice in the other. What a damn fool. Forty years old, and I'd never had an orgasm. I had two kids, but I'd never had an orgasm. So that's when the craziness started. I'd hang out at the singles spots. I came on to anyone, even the bartenders. It was easy. Guys are all horny. They were glad to accommodate me. But it was nothing. I felt terrible. And I still never had an orgasm. So okay, it was my fault, I decided. I was frigid.

"Then I met Howard. He was transferred to my office from another state. I'm a secretary at an insurance company. Well, Howard was management, but he was so nice to me. He said I was the best, the smartest secretary he had even seen, and he meant it. We started having coffee, then lunch, then 'working late,' if you know what I mean. He's married, too, so we did the classic thing. We went to a motel. Holy cow! You never forget the first time! I am definitely not frigid, believe you me. And after that I never wanted or needed another man. I'm still married, Howard is still married, and Howard and I are still lovers. In 1965 I couldn't have even pictured this. Life is strange. But Howard and I will be together forever. He says he kissed Sleeping Beauty and I came to life for him. And he's absolutely right."

Actually, the appeal of having one lover for a lifetime, rather than a series of trivial affairs, is not hard to understand. The women who kiss in the shadows all conveyed to me a sense of feeling special and cherished by their lovers, without ever having to give up the delicious excitement of romance. The very language these women use to describe their lovers betrays the fact that the connection is a kind of perpetual, giddy state which Helen Fisher calls "infatuation" and psychologist Dorothy Tennov has dubbed "limerance." This is the heart-thudding, brain-numbing, walking-on-air condition that occurs when human beings first fall in love, but that rarely lasts a lifetime, let alone more than about two years—presumably because it is both exhausting and distracting. However, Helen Fisher points out that "lovers who see each other irregularly, because of some barrier like an ocean or a wedding ring from another person, can sometimes sustain that smitten feeling for . . . years."

The reason may even be rooted in the chemistry of the brain. The work of psychiatrist Michael Liebowitz of the New York State Psychiatric Institute has shown that a substance called phenylethylamine (PEA) which causes feelings of elation and excitement may play a part in the experience of infatuation. (Interestingly this substance is also in chocolate, the quintessential lover's gift.) Liebowitz postulates that after a period of time the brain becomes satiated with PEA, and as tolerance rises, the sensations formerly caused by this natural "drug" diminish. The lovers then move from the "high" of infatuation to a more comfortable and predictable state known as attachment—and the brain produces endorphins (short for "endogenous morphine"), giving the couple in question a kind of pleasant, dopey feeling instead of the mad PEA passion of their early years together.

However, if the lovers see each other only sporadically, a "shot" of the brain's PEA may well continue to provide a magnificent rush during every rendezvous, in a kind of same-time-next-year scenario that can stretch out over a lifetime. This is surely why the women I spoke with who have primarily romantic/sexual relationships with their lovers virtually never marry these men—not even when the women become widows and are free to do so. Most of these women admitted to me that they are fully aware that the intensity they feel with their lovers could never exist full-time. It is too draining, too all-encompassing. It would not permit them to think of their children or other family members, let alone getting the laundry done. In fact, the heady experience of romantic love may even make a woman forget to eat, which is surely why so many women reported to me that they lost weight as soon as their lover relationships became intense.

Most of these women told me that they knew that ending their current marriages to marry their lovers would be dangerous. They may not be aware of the psychological dynamics or the brain chemistry involved, but they know instinctively that their lovers constitute glamour and sex and yearning and that the relationships could never survive if they were subjected to the demands of full-time togetherness. In effect, a woman in this situation knows she can't marry the mirage. What she has really created is a kind of ongoing fairy tale, in which the white knight who rescues her from the drudgery of her daily life remains a perfect illusion, and the story is always in a state of suspended animation, a sort of freeze-frame at the moment of happily ever after. And so, unlike real-life royals such as Princess Diana and the Duchess of York, these women never have to find out what life in the palace is truly all about.

"It's hard to feel wanton passion about a man when he squeezes the toothpaste from the middle of the tube, leaves dirty dishes in the sink, and tracks mud across the kitchen floor," said Mildred, now seventy-four, widowed for five years, and still seeing her lover of thirty years, but only about once a month, as has always been their custom. "Why spoil a beautiful relationship by turning it into a marriage? Leonard has always been my dream man, and I don't want to change anything just because my husband died. My heart still flutters when the phone rings and Leonard is on the other end of the line. But then, I've never had to sit and watch him watch Monday night football. I've never had to put his socks in the hamper. There are some things I'd rather not do."

Women like Mildred who married back when the role of "wife" involved putting aside personal needs and dreams and placing a man front and center in her life frequently vow never to get themselves into that kind of trap again. Remember that thirty years ago, when Mildred began her relationship with Leonard, she was forty-four, had been married for twenty-three years, and had just caught a whiff of the fresh air of the new feminism. And so she was perfectly happy not to be Leonard's wife. Why should she do his laundry, cook his meals, and make his bed? In her relationship with him, she was loved by invitation, not obligation, and Leonard most certainly didn't feel "entitled" to more of her than she was willing to give. So Mildred stayed with her safe, financially stable husband and did *his* laundry, and at the same time she kept up her adjunct romance with Leonard. Life, she says, was finally just as she wanted it.

Similarly, a woman I'll call Emma—spry and handsome at seventy-one—is a septuagenarian with a healthy sex drive and no desire to tie the knot with her long-term lover. A devout Christian from a small town in Ohio, she married at twenty-four, gave birth to four children, and then, just after her tenth wedding anniversary, met the man who eventually became her lover. For ten years she held the attraction at bay, except for an occasional assignation. Then, when the sexual revolution got under way, she finally gave in to her desires. The resulting wildly passionate, highly erotic liaison has lasted for twenty-seven years. Her children call him Uncle Bill, and he's always been a friend of the family. Actually, a fair number of the wives in my sample, particularly those in small towns, mentioned that their lovers frequented their homes and were known as uncle. Many of the wives also said that they were a part of their lovers' lives in a similar way and that they were called auntie by the children. Some were even godmothers for their lovers' children. But like Emma, these women still want to keep their lovers at a distance.

"Bill helped with my husband's funeral," says Emma. "I love him so much. But goodness knows, I'd never think of marrying him, not even if his wife died. She's quite frail, by the way, and in a nursing home. Anyway, my husband left me well set financially, and I'm fine living alone. I take my meals when I please. I putter in the garden or read or whatever I like. Land sakes, I've earned this time to myself! So Bill and I will go on the way we always have, making love when the mood strikes and living our separate lives. Of course, this is all so much easier now that his two children and my four are all grown and out of the house, and I'm alone. Looking back, I'm amazed that we've kept our secret all these years in this little town. We go to the same church, the same Rotary Club, everything. But where there's a will there's a way."

Indeed, there is. Just ask Carol, who is right in the middle of the life stage Emma remembers as being the most complicated. At forty-three Carol has been married for twenty years and is the mother of two teenagers. Her husband is a respected physician in their close-knit upstate New York community, and she is a full-time homemaker. Her lover, Keith, is a family friend, a dentist. His wife is a friend of Carol's, and his children have always been friends with her children. Yet Carol and Keith have managed to keep their steamy, surreptitious sex life a secret for the past eight years. Here is Carol's story, just as she told it to me:

"I had done some heavy petting in high school and college, but I was technically a virgin when I married Ron. I was twenty-three and he was twenty-five, and he admitted that he had slept with a fancy call girl once on a dare from his fraternity brothers, but he said that other than that he had no experience. I'm not being sarcastic, but I didn't find that hard to believe. For one thing, Ron is a workaholic, and even when we were dating on campus, I practically had to pry him away from his books to get him to go anywhere. And between you and me, he really seems to have a low sex drive. Oh, he enjoys sex, but I mean he doesn't need it all that often. About every three or four weeks. That is seriously our 'schedule,' and I don't even think he realizes it.

"Now, I am aware that complaining about not getting much sex could seem really picky of me since Ron is the kind of husband plenty of women would kill for. I mean, he's good-looking and he makes plenty of money. He's fantastic with the kids, and he's a deacon in the church and a member of the school board. Jeez, when I say all that, he sounds perfect! Sometimes I think about women trying to hang in there and bring up kids alone. I know two women whose ex-husbands don't send the child support. I also think about women with guys who put them down all the time or beat them or play power games with money, and I know I should count my blessings and be satisfied.

"Then again, where is it written that we have to settle for less than the best in any area of life? And believe me, Keith, the man I've been seeing on the side for eight years, is definitely the best when it comes to lovemaking. To be blunt, he has a very large penis. I'm sure you've read all that stuff about how penis size doesn't mean anything, but that's baloney. With Keith I feel, well, filled up, and I can have one orgasm after another—almost with no break in between. I just can't find the words to describe how this feels. And Keith loves giving me so much pleasure, having me writhe and scream and come again and again. It's fantastic. He says he reaches places my husband never touched, and sometimes he'll say, 'If Ron could see you now!'

"He doesn't really mean it in a bad way. He's like a superstar in bed, and he knows it. Think about this. Some people are born with gifts: They are born to be great baseball players or singers or ballet dancers. They have everything it takes, including the special physical requirements: a natural pitching arm, a gorgeous voice, a perfectly proportioned body, or whatever. Why can't we accept that the same is true for lovers? Keith has the drive, the skill—and trust me, he has the equipment to go with it.

"But I'm getting way ahead of myself. You wanted to know how this all started and how we make everything work. Okay, Ron and I met Keith and his wife, Glenda, ten years ago at a dinner party given by mutual friends. We were all thirtyish, the men were establishing their practices—as I said, Ron is a family practitioner and Keith is a dentist—and Glenda and I were both home with little kids. So we all hit it off, and Glenda and I started doing stuff together, taking the kids to the zoo and so on. My son, Jimmy, was five, and my daughter, Heather, was three. Glenda had two boys, six-year-old Kevin and four-year-old Gregory. Anyway, everybody got along great, and pretty soon we started sharing a baby-sitter, with the kids sleeping over at one house or the other, and Ron and I and Keith and Glenda would double-date.

"We never did anything all that exciting since there are only two movie theaters in town and one crummy diner that stays open until midnight. There's a billiards parlor, but it's become a teen hangout. So usually we would see a movie and then go home for a drink. Sometimes if there was nothing good at the theaters, we would just rent a video and go to whichever house the kids weren't staying at, and we'd make popcorn and snuggle up on the couch.

"I have to be honest, though. There was something between Keith and me from the very beginning, some kind of animal attraction. Neither one of us acted on it, given the friendship situation we were in, but it was there. To me, he is the sexiest man alive. For one thing, he has an intoxicating scent. It's his personal scent. No cologne from a bottle could make a man smell like that, trust me. And yet I noticed all along that Glenda didn't seem to react to him. He'd put his arm around her when they were sitting on the couch, and she wouldn't pull away, but she wouldn't cuddle up either. I mean, I wasn't even the one he was touching, and I got goose bumps!

"So we all went along like that for about two years. Then one Friday evening the four of us went to see a movie, and we sat down in this order: Glenda four seats in from the aisle, then Keith, then me, and then Ron on the aisle. I guess we arranged ourselves like that most of the time, but on this particular night, in this pitch-black theater, with some torrid love scene on the screen, Keith put his hand on top of mine on the armrest between us. Oh, my God! I am not exaggerating when I say that I was instantly aroused—but this was much stronger than I had ever known before. Then I felt as though I couldn't breathe and I got panicky. I wanted to run out of the theater, but there was Ron in the aisle seat. Not that I would have run out anyway, not that I would have made a public scene, but I'm just trying to tell you that I felt trapped, hemmed in, while I was hot and throbbing in all the right places. I swear, if I had simply crossed my legs tight, I would have had an orgasm right then and there.

"This all took place in a split second, and then I got myself together and pulled my hand from under Keith's. In some crazy way I was afraid Ron would know what had happened, and so I reached out to hold his hand. He took my hand and gave it a little squeeze. And I felt nothing. No, that's not true. I felt what I have always felt with Ron. Safe. Protected. Cherished, even. But definitely no fireworks.

"I was afraid to look Keith in the eye the whole rest of the evening. Actually, I was afraid to look anybody in the eye. I had done nothing yet, but I felt as though I had betrayed not only Ron but Glenda, who had become my best friend. I also thought about my children, whom I love like life itself. I wanted them to grow up respecting me and to have good values themselves. How could I ever justify letting my emotions get the better of me? I'd have to lie to the kids and to everyone. The thought made me sick, and I swore that nothing could make me act on my physical desire for Keith.

"Then, about two weeks later, I had a dental emergency. A gold inlay fell out and exposed a nerve, and I was in terrible pain. Our regular family dentist, an elderly man we had started with long before we met Keith, was out of town, and his service said that it was Keith who was on call. I really had no choice. I couldn't wait for three days in that kind of pain. So there I was, lying back in a dentist's chair, one side of my mouth numb with Novocaine, and the whole rest of me throbbing just like in the movie theater, while Keith leaned over me, his face so close, his scent everywhere. Then at one point he sent the hygienist out to get something, and he whispered, 'Meet me back here at six-thirty.' I just kind of nodded. It was as though I were on automatic pilot.

"I went home and called Ron at his office. I told him my tooth was fine, that Keith had put in a temporary filling, and the new inlay would be ready soon. Then I told him that I had forgotten there was a meeting of the American Association of University Women at the library. I said I had been meaning to join. Actually, there *was* a meeting. I had seen it advertised in the library newsletter. So I put the newsletter on the coffee table, open to that page. Of course, Ron could have gone over to the library to see if I was there, but I knew he wouldn't. He had no reason not to trust me. In fact, he sounded pleased that I wanted to join the AAUW, and he said he'd take the kids to McDonald's. Good. The other side of town from Keith's office. I made a mental note to call and join the AAUW the following week. It sounds so terrible to tell all this, but I was driven. I couldn't stop myself.

"I parked in the library lot and walked the six blocks to Keith's office. Thank God nobody saw me. It's a small town, and at the dinner hour I'll bet that ninety-eight percent of the population is saying grace and serving chicken. So I arrived at Keith's office, and he had been watching for me through the frosted glass. I wanted to turn and run, but I didn't. He opened the door, and I slipped inside. He said that he had told Glenda he had late office hours because of an emergency and that this was not unusual, so she would never suspect.

"He took me in his arms, and the rest is history. Once you have known pleasure like that, life is simply not complete without it. Keith is amazing. In one lovemaking session he can get a second erection within a very short time after the first one and have another orgasm. And he can wait, prolonging the whole thing for me, letting me have multiples, and then, well, joining me at the last minute. We are this virtuoso couple, a world-class team. I know it's wrong, but I don't want to stop!

"So it hasn't been all that hard to pull off. I leave the AAUW meetings early sometimes. Also, I joined an evening aerobics class, and I go to most of the classes, so everybody knows me and would vouch for my being there. But I can manage at least one evening a month to go to Keith's office instead of class. And he just keeps telling Glenda that he's working late. Also, I was on the pill for a while, and then both men had vasectomies, so we're safe on that front—as long as nobody has AIDS. So far so good.

"I don't really feel guilty. Well, there was one night two years ago when I got home after making love with Keith, and the kids were in bed and Ron was in the mood. I hadn't taken a shower. That did upset me. He wanted oral sex, which is rare for him, and I just whispered that I had to go to the bathroom, and I washed the best I could. He never guessed, but that was one moment when I felt terrible guilt.

"Then, too, I can't deny that I worry about the kids. They are fifteen and thirteen by now, and it won't be long before they both have a social life and drivers' licenses. They are not necessarily going to be home eating dinner every evening, and even now they are long past thinking it's a big thrill to go to McDonald's with Daddy. If they were ever in town and saw me sneaking into Keith's office, I would die. I can't even imagine what I would do, how I would explain myself.

"And of course, I don't ever want Ron to know. He would be destroyed. And rightly so. What did he ever do to deserve a wife who makes love to his best friend? I'm sure he'd want a divorce. He's a very proud man. And then where would I be? I'm totally dependent on him financially. And you can bet that Keith would never leave Glenda and the kids for me. Not that Ron wouldn't give me a fair settlement, I'm sure, but even so, I'd have to work, and I wouldn't know where to begin. I was an English major in college, but I don't even have a teaching certificate. I can type, but I don't know word processors. Oh, brother.

"So I'm crazy. What is it that makes a person take such risks? What is this attraction between Keith and me? There must be some explanation. Because we can't be the only ones, can we?"

———

No, indeed. As I heard time after time, whether from a black woman who is a church organist in Tennessee, married to a black construction worker and in love with her husband's best friend . . . or from the high-powered matrimonial lawyer in Manhattan, a Jewish woman married to an agnostic and in love with an Irish Catholic . . . or from the apple-cheeked kindergarten teacher, born and bred in Kansas, just like the farmer she married and the farmer she sees on the side, more and more postpill, postfeminist women are living double lives that could never even have been considered as short a time ago as the fifties, let alone the turn of the century. Back then, when every sexual encounter meant a possible pregnancy, and when complications of childbirth kept the average age of death for women at about forty, the "joy of sex" wasn't a phrase that could trip lightly off any female tongue. That was an era when Oscar Wilde, who wrote, "I can resist everything except temptation," was speaking for men only. Yet today legions of women would heartily agree with him.

And anthropologist Helen Fisher, looking at overwhelming sexual attraction from a Darwinian perspective, points out that "sexual beings are like ornamented Christmas trees, bearing an arsenal of accoutrements to win their fortunes and their futures through copulation and reproduction." More specifically, she reminds us that Carol's personal experience of great pleasure with a genitally well-endowed man is not unusual. In fact, Fisher points out that not only humans but many other species have "exceptionally elaborate penises" and that "scientists think these evolved specifically because females chose those males with elaborate, sexually stimulating genitals." As for human beings, Fisher agrees with Carol that the penis size matters. "A fat phallus distends the muscles of the outer third of the vaginal canal and pulls on the hood of the clitoris, creating exciting friction, making the contractions of orgasm more intense," Fisher contends.

That being so, however, how do we explain the fact that Carol's lover, Keith, never excited his own wife as much as he did Carol? As a psychologist I feel certain that Keith selected a wife who was a "good" woman, one who never responded in a bawdy fashion to his advances or, he hoped, to anyone else's. He felt safe and socially correct with her and simply sought his sexual release outside that union—a story as old as time itself. Of course, we'll never know Glenda's whole story. Maybe she had a lover of her own. And perhaps her attraction to him had nothing to do with his penis size. There are, after all, plenty of other factors that contribute to the chemistry of love.

In fact, there is strong evidence that one of the most irresistible lures between lovers is controlled by the sense of smell. As Helen Fisher details in *Anatomy of Love,* almost a century ago French naturalist Jean Henri Fabre, experimenting with emperor moths, established the existence of pheromones—powerful natural perfumes, in effect "odor lures," that attract potential mates. Since then the pheromones of more than 250 insect species and many other animals as well have been isolated. And while no scientific evidence exists to prove whether the scent of human males can trigger desire in human females (or vice versa), an experiment performed by a team at the Monell Chemical Senses Center in Philadelphia in 1986 did establish that exposure to concentrated "male essence" stimulated normal menstrual cycling and thus ovulation in the female subjects—an important factor in successful reproduction. Beyond that, everyone knows that "scent memory" is extremely potent. A whiff of some odor associated with a past event can bring back the moment with astonishing clarity. And so for people like Carol and Keith, scent may indeed play a part in pulling them toward each other.

But the truth is, human sexual attraction is still a mystery. A great many women in my sample talked about love at first sight. One woman said, "That's how it was for me with my lover. Not with my husband. That was just a conscious decision. But with my lover it was instant."

In this regard psychologist John Money talks about a "lovemap," a sort of guidebook in the brain, imprinted there from our earliest years. It consists of everything we know about loving, including scent, sight, the sound of a voice. In adulthood a person may fall in love at first sight with someone who calls up those impressions.

All speculation aside, however, attractions like the one Keith and Carol experienced turn out to be not at all uncommon among the people who spoke with me. Listen to a few others:

═══

❥**Marla, fifty-four:** Mother of three, married for thirty years to Neil, sexually involved with Ed from her eighth year of marriage until about six months ago. "He just couldn't take the double life anymore, the stress of sneaking around. That's what he says. But he'll be back. He won't be able to stay away. I swear, we are physically addicted to each other. I'll never forget the day we met. We were at a neighborhood block party, and there was a square dance caller. Ed was my 'corner,' and when we switched partners and he put his arm around my waist, BOOM, I knew we were hooked."

＝＝＝＝

❧Julia, fifty-seven: Mother of two, married for thirty-two years to Tom, sexually involved with Paul for five years. "I faked orgasms with my husband from the wedding night on. He never noticed. We stopped sleeping together about ten years ago, and we've never discussed this. Otherwise, the marriage is normal and good. I had never even thought about having an affair. Then, when the children were grown, I stepped up my volunteer work and got very involved as a member of the board of directors for the local arts council. I met Paul at the annual fund-raising gala, and when I danced with him, I experienced sensations I didn't even know the human body was capable of. We held off for a few months, and then it started. He's marvelous. Now I know what an orgasm is! Paul makes me feel warm, graceful, tingling, as if all my nerve endings were exposed in the best sense. I feel fortunate to have found this man. But I could never leave my husband. He's a good man; the children love him; he has provided for me all these years. In a very real sense I'm an economic captive. But I also don't want to disrupt everything and I want Tom and me to be Grandpa and Grandma together. So I'll keep my sex as a side dish."

＝＝＝＝

❧Tammy, thirty-five: Two children, widowed at eighteen, now married for eleven years to Norman, sexually involved for six years with Ralph. "I know that what I'm doing is wrong, and I know that it is a terrible thing. And sometimes when I sing in the choir in church, I look out over the congregation and see Ralph and his wife and I think, How could someone like me, a really good Christian, have allowed this to happen? But I can't give him up. I also can't leave my husband. I just wouldn't do that to him. My husband had prostate cancer a few years ago. He had surgery and everything, and he's okay now, but I know he needs me. This is very painful. Sometimes I hate myself. It is very difficult for someone who was brought up with a strong religious streak to live like this. I am a really good person. A decent person. But I've tried to break up with Ralph, and then we'll be playing cards—me and my husband and Ralph and his wife—and he'll play footsie and I have to have him. He reminds me a lot of my first husband, who died in a trucking accident when I was eighteen and six months pregnant. He was my greatest love. I still miss him. And Ralph kind of eases that for me. Especially the sex. It's just unbelievable. With my current husband, it's so-so. But my husband is a good guy. He has adopted my daughter from my first marriage, and we have a son of our own. My husband has a good job in the tobacco industry. I'll never leave him, like I said. I just ask God how this happened. There must be a reason. I'm just not smart enough to figure it out, I guess.

"I have a white leather Bible that my parents gave me when I was confirmed. I was twelve years old, and I loved that Bible. At the beginning it has these beautiful pages with flowers around the border and fancy lettering, and you're supposed to fill in your family information. It has pages for weddings and births and deaths. It doesn't have pages for divorces. Divorces are just out of the question. Of course, it doesn't have pages for affairs either. I know I'm not supposed to be doing this. There's not a day that I don't feel bad about it. But I'm glad you asked me to talk. I feel a little better now. I never told anyone before, and I never will again."

═══

❥**Kim, forty-five:** Two children, married for twenty-five years to Victor, sexually involved for fifteen years with Mike. "My parents are first-generation immigrants from Japan, and all during my childhood I knew I was supposed to grow up and marry Victor. I never objected. Arranged marriages looked like a good idea to me. You got a nice man, financially stable, from a nice family. Victor was heir to his family's restaurant, and I started working there, too. So I married Victor. I was a virgin, and I became a dutiful wife, but I didn't enjoy sex. It seemed like just one more household chore.

"Then, when my first son was four and my second son was two, a customer came into the restaurant on an evening when I was acting as the hostess. He looked to be in his late twenties—I was just thirty at the time—and he was wearing tight jeans and a white T-shirt. He had the most incredible build. Those biceps and those pecs! I knew he worked out. And he had a chiseled face, a kind of James Dean look. I could barely speak, barely offer him a seat. Then I realized he was staring at me, too. I always dressed like a traditional geisha girl when I was working; it was a gimmick, but the customers loved it, and the restaurant was very elegant with traditional decor and low lighting. Anyway, we just stood there looking into each other's eyes. To make a long story short, he came back three nights in a row, and we soon found ways to be alone together. The sex was thrilling from the beginning, and we've been very experimental over the years, so the glow has never faded. We see each other about once a month. The only thing that has put a damper on this is a terror of getting pregnant. Obviously, I can't give birth to a child with Western eyes! I was on the pill for a while, but then my doctor recommended against it. We've been using a combination of a diaphragm and a condom. And I pay attention to when I'm probably ovulating, since I'm very regular. But I can't wait until menopause, when my lover and I can relax and really pull out all the stops."

=====

❧**Martha, seventy:** Three children, married for fifty-one years to Clarence, sexually involved with Sam for fourteen years, until his death. "I got married at the age of nineteen because I was pregnant. In 1940 you either got a back-alley abortion, or got sent away to a home and gave the baby up for adoption, or got married really fast and said the baby was premature. I chose the latter mostly because my boyfriend was rich and willing to marry me and I wanted to get away from my parents. I was an only child, and my mother was very pushy but also very condescending, and my father was just there. He never got involved.

"So we had an apartment that my husband's parents paid for while they also paid for him to finish school. We had twin beds. I'm not kidding! My husband thought that was proper. He came right out and said that a married woman, a mother, shouldn't be 'too raunchy.' I wonder if he went to a prostitute or had a lover. I suppose so. He needed a bad girl, and he made me be the good girl.

"Life went on like that until our silver anniversary, when I was forty-four years old. We had a huge party in our lovely home in Wilton, Connecticut. Clarence was a very successful stockbroker by then, and I was a very proper middle-aged lady, with three grown children and one grandchild. Well, one of the guests was a gentleman I had never met before, a colleague of my husband's. I won't deny that I was taken aback when we were introduced. He looked amazingly like Sidney Poitier, and he was impeccably groomed and thoroughly cultured. Remember, this was 1965, still a very racially tense time, and it was unusual to have a black man come to Wilton. But that wasn't all. I honestly had an instant reaction to him. My scalp prickled. I assumed I was having my first hot flash. Actually, I was experiencing sexual arousal for the first time in my life.

"After that I saw Sam several times at business functions, dinners where the wives went along, and one evening—at a formal function with place cards—we were seated next to each other. We never said anything outright, but we each knew what we wanted. He slipped me his business card with a date and time and address scribbled on the back. I nodded.

"The rendezvous was a week later, at a secluded country inn on a Tuesday afternoon. I don't know how he got off work, but I had no problem meeting him. I always came and went as I pleased during the day. I played bridge, went shopping, had lunch with my girlfriends. The housekeeper always started dinner anyway. Well, that afternoon I had my first orgasm. I'll never forget it. It was fireworks, the Fourth of July,

New Year's Eve, and champagne all at the same time. So Sam and I had our little assignations like that for years and years. It was glorious, and yes, of course, I fell in love. But you can see that I could never have left Clarence for Sam.

"Then one afternoon, during the afterglow, lying there with our arms around each other, Sam whispered, 'There won't be many more times like this, my darling.' I froze. What was he telling me? But it was worse than I could ever have imagined. Sam was dying. He had an inoperable brain tumor. They gave him six months to live. He lasted four. Clarence and I went to the funeral. Sam had a large, extended family, and they were all there weeping and hugging one another, and I was just an outsider, an acquaintance paying a courtesy call on my husband's arm. I'll never get over it as long as I live. But the truth is, I never would have left Clarence for Sam even if he had lived."

———

And so it goes, the details differing but the essence of the story remaining the same for woman after woman. Not one wife even considered divorce, and in one way or another they all were convinced that their affairs helped rather than hurt their marriages. And while they stressed that sex with their lovers was magnificent, very often giving them pleasure they had never experienced with their husbands, they did continue to sleep with their husbands.

A few of the wives had gone through a period of postmarital promiscuity, yet none of those who did so had enjoyed that phase. Rather, they had felt empty and afraid. Only when they found the men who would become their long-term lovers did they find the satisfaction, both physical and emotional, which they had been seeking so desperately. For indeed, while this group of wives saw sex as the prime reason for the long-term affairs, they all had deep emotional bonds with their lovers as well, and the emotional aspect of the relationships had in every case preceded the sexual. Also, even the wives who went through a promiscuous period were ultimately faithful to their long-term lovers.

And they were masterful at the business of keeping their affairs secret. Actually, while scores of wives did volunteer to talk with me for this book, many more wives filled out anonymous questionnaires but shied away at the last minute from actual interviews. They said they couldn't bring themselves to risk recognition. They said their lives would be ruined if anyone ever found out or even suspected.

The wives who did speak with me, however, said that they trusted that I would disguise them and that they actually were burning to share their secrets. They said they hoped other people could learn something from this. One woman said, "Why is it that women have not always passed on from one generation to the next the truth about love and sex and marriage? Oh, sure, we've become much more open about talking about stuff like incest, child molestation, battering, philandering, emotional abuse, alcoholism, and drugs. But most mothers still don't talk frankly with their daughters. My mother taught me how to fix up, wear makeup, catch a man. But then I wasn't supposed to like sex. What kind of crazy, mixed-up message is that anyway?"

And another wife pointed out women still make great efforts to present their husbands as perfect, even though this image may be far from the truth. "I'm glad this story is being told," she said. "I always wondered if I was the only one, and now you're saying there are a lot of us. We are not bad people. We are trying to make sense out of something that doesn't make sense. I hope my daughter has a chance to live differently. I hope she waits until she's thirty to even think about getting married, and I hope that when she says she's in love, she's got her eyes wide open. Because I certainly didn't, and look what a mess it got me in. I got married at nineteen, and I have to live with that for the rest of my life."

This sentiment was echoed by almost all the wives, whether they are young, middle-aged, or elderly; wellborn, working-class, or immigrants; educated or not; Christian, Jewish, or Eastern Orthodox. They hail from cities and small towns, coast to coast, and everywhere in between.

This diversity, however, belies some striking similarities among these women. For example, many of the women married young and in haste, and most are economically dependent on their husbands, particularly if there are children involved. Of course, another discernible common thread among the women who maintain long-term, two-track love lives to fill sexual needs is that they have quite simply succumbed to the ancient, relentless undertow of human sexual attraction itself. Yet just why these particular women at this particular time have split themselves in the Wife/Wench syndrome—maintaining their good wife/mother status while concurrently engaging in "wanton" relationships with their lovers—appears to me to have roots in their reasons for marrying in the first place. As I have noted, the majority of the women in my sample said they were "in love," but on closer examination there was no universal definition for that phrase. The women we have met in this chapter gave specific reasons for the initial appeal of their husbands, and they were almost all on the same note: "He was decisive. . . . He wanted to take care of me. . . . He provided security and stability." Ironically, though, these once-desired traits turned negative with the years, and the women complained: "He's taking over my life and making all my decisions for me. . . . I have to go to him for every penny. . . . There's no spontaneity, no fun in our lives." These women then react to their pseudoparent husbands by having a kind of belated adolescent sexual rebellion. In effect, they claim their own bodies, saying to themselves, "I own myself. My body belongs to me. I can share it with anyone I want to. It's mine, and I don't have to ask permission from anyone." It is poignant to note that for many of these women their bodies are in effect the only things they own and can control. This is particularly true for those wives who seem to lead charmed lives with well-to-do husbands but who are actually economic captives in master/slave marriage relationships.

The fact that these women came to this stage of development so late in life is testimony to the conflicting messages about sexuality which this culture still sends. On the one hand, sex is glamorized, and sexy models are used to sell everything from cars to soft drinks. Yet on the other hand—all the talk of the sexual revolution in the seventies notwithstanding—women are still told that "good girls" don't enjoy sex. I think of the seventeen-year-old daughter of a friend of mine who came home in tears from a week's retreat with her church youth group. The girl had been severely reprimanded for holding hands with her boyfriend "in public" on the way from the meeting lodge to the cafeteria. She was told that "nice girls don't do bad things like that." The young man in question was not similarly chastised. This is the kind of conditioning that leads many women to suppress their sexuality in order to be seen as good by their parents and later by their husbands. This unfortunate mind-set keeps wives from responding honestly in the marriage bed, and indeed, many of these wives have unconsciously selected mates who are just as uncomfortable with the issue of sexuality as they are. Yet when a wife in this situation meets a man who becomes the "spark" which ignites her and makes her glow, she bifurcates into the Wife/Wench, a kind of double personality who is "good" with the good man and "bad" with the illicit lover.

Yet while these women seem to have no need or desire to integrate the two parts of themselves, they do feel some guilt over the situation. The guilt, however, comes not from the illicit sexual activity itself but from the fact that they take their husbands' money, let the men provide food, clothing, and shelter for the whole family, while the women give their true sexual selves to their lovers. "I feel like an emotional whore," one wife told me. "My husband is a perfectly nice man. He's a good provider. He's a good father. I'm a full-time homemaker, so I'm totally dependent on him to bring home the bacon. In return, I'm a very good wife, a traditional wife. But let's face it. I'm cheating on him. I'd be lying if I said this doesn't pain me. What gets me through this is that the person I am when I'm with my lover is not even a person my husband knows. He wouldn't even recognize me. It's that different. So I tell myself that my husband is getting everything he ever bargained for in a wife and that there's just more to me than that, so I take the extra stuff elsewhere. But yeah, I feel guilty."

Still, the guilt is not enough to keep this woman and many others from acting on their desires. And certainly, for those women who are not economically dependent on their husbands, the sexual liaison is frequently not guilt-provoking at all. Listen to the story of Elizabeth, a highly educated career woman who married late and could easily have managed on her own financially:

———

"I'm aware that a lot of the women I grew up with were spoon-fed the business about being the perfect wife and mother, the fifties thing. I'm forty-five, a boomer from Illinois, but my parents were not typical. My mother was a high school principal, a very powerful position for a woman in that day and age. She had a master's degree. My father was a lawyer, and I was an only child. They kind of treated me like a little adult, taking me to fancy restaurants with them and to the theater in Chicago. And they always told me I was smart and could be anything I wanted to be. So I decided to become a doctor. My parents also told me there was no rush to get married, that I could get started in my career and still have plenty of time for a personal life. After all, my mother was thirty-five and my father thirty-eight when I was born, so there was the perfect example.

"Anyway, let's fast forward to Harvard Medical School, where I met Peter. There's not much leeway for a social life when you're doing rounds for your residency, but he and I figured out right away that we were perfect for each other. He liked the fact that I was determined to make it in a man's world, and he said that the last thing he wanted was some dependent little woman. He had seen that scenario with his mother and father, and he hated it. So we got married when we were both almost thirty, and we both had good practices established in Newton, a suburb of Boston, which we picked because of the excellent school district. We decided to start a family when we were thirty-five. I got pregnant right away, and we had twins, a boy and girl. We joked about how efficient we had been, just like Margaret Thatcher. So we hired a live-in nanny, and I had my tubes tied, and that was that.

"Now all along our sex life had been limited, given our hectic schedules, but it had been pretty good. I had nothing much to compare it to, having had only two brief encounters before I got married. But Peter was very thoughtful, wanting me to have pleasure, and he was also romantic. You know, he always remembered my birthday and our anniversary, and he'd bring flowers or jewelry. I treated him well, too, and he loved it when I'd take him out to dinner and pick up the check myself. He was always very flattered, and very proud of me. I'd overhear him bragging about me to his friends.

"So then, one February, when I was forty, I went to a convention in another state. My specialty is pediatrics, and there were going to be the top people in the field there. The twins were almost five, and I had never been away from them before, so I felt very strange and lonely when I got on the plane. But the minute we landed I was in heaven. I remember riding in the limousine on the way to the hotel, and thinking, This is my reward. I mean, I suddenly felt as if I had done nothing but work, work, work since kindergarten. I'm only half joking. I could read when I was three, and my parents put me in a progressive private school for the gifted where we did second-grade stuff when we were only five years old.

"So it was about four o'clock when we got to the hotel, and everybody was planning to change into a bathing suit and go for a dip in the pool or the ocean before dressing for dinner. I had bought a new suit for the occasion, black with a magenta V in front, and I remember looking at myself in the mirror and thinking, Not bad for an old girl with two kids. I do ride a stationary bike every day and play tennis in the summer, so I've kept in pretty good shape.

"I wrapped a beach towel around my waist, put on a sun hat and sunglasses, and walked out to the elevator bank. And there he was. Adonis personified, at least as far as I was concerned. And all he had on were his trunks. His robe was over his arm. He held out his hand and said, 'I'm Doctor White, from Virginia.'

"The convention was only going to last four days. I don't have to tell you that I wanted to spend time with Doctor White before the meetings were over. That didn't prove to be a problem. He wanted to see me, too. We've been seeing each other now for five years, about twice a year. Our spouses are busy with their own lives. So we can meet each other with no problem. I pay for my own travel, of course, and I do everything I can to keep my affair in its place, secret. My husband is not aware of what is going on. I would never want to hurt him.

"You know, I think my affair has actually improved my marriage. Peter and I have much more inventive sex now that I know what it's all about. But sex with my lover will always be the best. There's just something perfect—a harmony, a sexual pas de deux. Still, I would never in a million years leave my husband for my lover. And he wouldn't leave his wife and kids either. You understand, I could support myself, so I don't need Peter in that sense. But in every other way we've built a life together. My lover is just a fantasy, really. I don't even want to know what it would be like to be married to him."

═══════

There's that familiar refrain again. These Wife/Wench women have managed to divide themselves neatly into the good wife and mother and the woman with a lover. As one woman said, "I flip a switch in my head. When I'm at home, cooking and cleaning and taking care of my kids, I am one person. Even when I'm in bed with my husband, I'm that person. Then, when I'm with my lover, I flip the switch, and I'm another kind of person, so totally sexual and free. A more authentic me. I don't really feel any conflict about this. I've learned to accept the situation. Because there's no other solution. I certainly have no intention of leaving my husband and destroying my children's lives. But I also have no intention of giving up my lover, now that I know how glorious sex can really be. On the other hand, I wouldn't marry my lover. I mean, then he'd be my husband, and it just wouldn't be the same. I just know it. It would spoil everything we have between us."

These Wife/Wench women, then, have a strong need to keep their "good" and "bad" selves separate, but because most often their husbands are contributing to the situation by imposing a Madonna/Whore standard, the wives also seem to understand—in a kind of twist on the old storybook scenario—that while a kiss may turn a frog into a prince, a marriage license might well break the spell and turn the prince into a frog. The wives fear that their lovers, should they become their husbands, would expect wifely behavior in bed, and the party would be over.

Yet while this aversion to marrying the lovers holds true for the wives whose lovers fill sexual needs, the situation is dramatically different for women whose lovers meet whatever emotional needs their husbands ignore. As one fifty-five-year-old woman put it: "Jim and I were drawn immediately and strongly to each other's intellect and sensibility. Had we hopped easily into bed, we'd probably have had a passionate relationship on the fringe of our real lives. But we admired each other's work, minds, emotions most of all. Frankly, that is far more dangerous . . . "

3

All Dressed Up and No Place to Grow

Hasty marriage seldom proveth well.

—William Shakespeare

When I got married to Corey at the age of twenty-three, I thought I was on the brink of the exciting life I had always dreamed of," Linda said with a rueful little laugh. "Well, nothing could have been farther from the truth. See, before I met Corey, I had graduated from the University of Michigan, and I was teaching French at a junior high school in a small town outside Detroit. But I wanted more than that. I wanted adventure, travel, excitement. Oh, eventually I wanted a couple of kids and the proverbial house with the picket fence. But I wanted to do some living, some exploring, some growing up first. Corey seemed like just the life partner for all of that."

Linda, a trim and attractive blonde at forty-three, spooned some sugar into her coffee and stirred it for a while, obviously collecting her thoughts. A chill rain was driving against the window of the little coffee shop we had ducked into. It was late March, and we were in Canada—

Windsor, Ontario, to be exact, across the river from Detroit. Linda had insisted that we leave the country before she would so much as whisper her tale of passionate intrigue, one that spanned more than a decade and, in her own words, "saved my marriage and my life."

"So anyway," she said, "to backtrack a little, Corey and I met when I went back to U of M one summer to take courses toward my master's degree. He was twenty-one, and he had just graduated. He was working in the bookstore and planning to go to grad school in the fall. His major was art history, and he did some painting himself. Also, he had spent his junior year in Paris. He was quite a romantic figure. I don't know what I pictured, really: eloping and living in Paris, where he would paint and I would write novels, or something like that. God, was I ever that young?"

She sipped her coffee, looking straight at me for the first time. "So I pushed and pushed for us to get married. My father and stepmother are middle-class, but certainly not wealthy, and I have two sisters, so I called my stepmother—who raised me from the age of ten after my own mother died—and I said, 'You don't have to give me a big wedding if you'll pay my grad school tuition and let me stay here and get this degree finished in one year instead of making me teach and spend the next zillion summers in school.' She talked it over with my dad, and he said okay, so I told Corey we were going for the blood tests and to get a license and we'd have a few friends and family and get married by a justice of the peace. This was now one week from the end of summer school. Corey just kind of shrugged and said that was fine. He had his own apartment, which I had all but moved into anyway, and we had been sleeping together for about a month. He seemed to like the idea of having me available all the time. He wanted oral sex a lot, which I wasn't crazy about, but you can see that I was consciously or unconsciously doing anything to get this guy—and to avoid going back to teaching those seventh graders."

She stopped for a moment, cocking her head pensively. "Am I giving you the impression that I didn't love Corey?" she asked. "I hope not. I mean, I not only loved him then but still love him now. He's got a lot going for him. But see, the life script I had in the back of my mind never even came close to happening. We both finished our master's degrees the next year, and then I took a teaching job in another Detroit suburb, and Corey came along to look for work. So now I had another classroomful of seventh graders, a little bit better salary than the one I had been making before, and an unemployed husband. Paris this was not."

The waitress poured us each a second cup of coffee, and Linda went on to explain that Corey finally took a job in an insurance company, but that he lasted there only a few years, and that this was to be a pattern that was to repeat itself throughout the marriage.

"Once, when he was employed and seemed to be doing really well, I got pregnant," Linda said. "Our daughter, who is now twelve, was born that July, and I was planning to stay home with her, but Corey got fired again, and so I was right back teaching in September. That was the worst period of my life. Corey was supposedly Mr. Mom, but the house was always a total wreck, the baby was crying for her bottle when I got home, and Corey was just oil painting to his heart's content—when he wasn't watching TV, that is. I would complain to my stepmother, and she'd do the old 'You made your bed, now lie in it' routine. I was going nuts with no one to talk to. I had some women friends, but you know how sometimes you put up a front? You don't want your marriage to be a failure. It's just so hard to admit that things are not going well.

"Also, I certainly wasn't about to tell anyone that our sex life had gotten really weird. The oral sex became a demand, and Corey is very large and I would gag. He wanted me to swallow when he came. If I refused, he would get nasty. This got to be a battleground, and the more I resisted, the more often he would force himself on me. I was miserable."

At this point a slow smile softened Linda's features, and I saw the tension drain out of her face. She relished a memory for a moment and then shared it with me. "One day, when I was supposed to stay after school for a French Club meeting, I slipped into the teachers' lounge for a cigarette, and somehow I just started sobbing and sobbing. I was alone, and I put my head down on the table. Then I felt a hand on my shoulder, very gentle, but I jumped out of my skin. I looked up and saw Mr. Roberts, the assistant principal. I felt like a total fool, and I fumbled in my purse for some tissues, but he handed me his handkerchief and didn't say a word until I could get myself together. I started laughing and crying at the same time because the situation was so embarrassing, but he smiled really sympathetically, and finally I just said I had some family problems and was sorry I had lost it at work. He said, 'You're only human,' in the kindest voice, and I honestly, physically felt my heart flutter. I fixed my makeup and went to the French Club meeting, but I knew he wasn't going to leave it at that. Especially since as I was going out the door, I said, 'Thank you so much, Mr. Roberts.' 'Bill,' he said, 'call me Bill.' "

Linda's smile was broad and radiant by now, and as if on cue, the rain had stopped and a slash of sunshine cut across our table. I suggested that we get the check and go for a walk while she told me the rest of her story. Outside in the brisk spring breeze Linda obviously began to enjoy getting all this off her chest once and for all. She said that Bill had stopped by her classroom the day after their first encounter, and then they began finding ways to meet for coffee or clandestine dinners. This wasn't easy for Linda, with her husband and daughter waiting at home, but fortunately Bill was flexible because even though he had been dating one woman fairly steadily for seven years, he was in fact a bachelor who could make his own hours. In any case, partly because of the time pressures and partly because of Linda's guilty reluctance to "really cheat on Corey," a full year went by this way before Bill and Linda ever slept together.

"The funny thing is," Linda said, "once we did have sex, I realized that the friendship, the emotional closeness, which we had always shared was the most important part of our relationship. You think you're still faithful to your husband just because you're not sleeping with someone else, but what I was getting from Bill all along was a kind of intimacy that is just as powerful as sex."

She flushed and smiled again. "Not that the sex hasn't been wonderful. Bill has always complimented me and made me feel equal to him. In a way the sex has been just like our conversations: stimulating, a two-way street, nobody dominating or making demands, both of us experiencing great pleasure."

We strolled in silence for a while, and then I asked Linda whether she had ever considered leaving Corey for Bill. "I've thought about it," she said softly, a little sadly. "He really wanted me to, about four years ago. But remember, I have a daughter. She adores her father. And to be honest, things have gotten better between Corey and me in every area, and I seriously credit my affair with that. I've matured a lot, I have much more self-respect, and I know that I'm good in bed. This all gave me the strength to stand up to Corey, to tell him that he was too demanding in bed and that he wasn't pulling his weight in the marriage. He was stunned, but we have worked out some compromises. We've even been to a counselor, which has really helped.

"For one thing, Corey got a job as a commercial artist with a small advertising company, and this time he doesn't have an attitude at work the way he always used to. He's been with the same company for six years. I think it's going to last this time. Also, he's better about helping with the housework and not nearly as domineering in bed."

There was a long pause. Linda let out a great sigh and finally said, "Anyway, Bill got married last June. His wife is someone new, not the woman he had been seeing for so long. He was tired of waiting for me. He says he loves her, and I can't deny that I'm jealous. Bill and I have slept together three times since his wedding, but it's not the same anymore. We both feel funny."

Will she stop seeing Bill? I wondered. "Oh, no!" she said quickly. "Probably we won't have sex anymore. It just doesn't feel right. But our friendship has always been the most important part, and that will go on as long as we live. We've grown up together over the last twelve years. Bill is as much a part of my life as Corey is. And I have no regrets. I'd probably be divorced right now if Bill hadn't rescued me from that moment which was the darkest night of my soul. I'll always, always love Bill. I've never admitted this to myself before, but I wish—and this is such a terrible thing to say—but I wish I had met Bill first."

━━━━━

Linda is in good company. Of the married women in my sample, the 31 percent who are seeing other men because they fill *emotional* vacuums rather than primarily *sexual* needs find the adjunct relationships more satisfying and profound than the marriages. The pattern which I saw emerging was that these women and their husbands, like Linda and Corey, were all less than fully developed people when they got married. Whether the couples tied the knot because society seemed to expect them to, or because they were running away from bad home situations, or because of unplanned pregnancies, the fact is that they set up conjugal housekeeping long before they had finished the social and psychological tasks of becoming adults. In this regard I think about a certain shy nineteen-year-old on her wedding day in 1981. Diana Spencer, a secondary school dropout who worked as a nursery school aide, was so nervous when she said her vows that she got her husband's name wrong, but she became Princess Diana, the future queen of England, anyway. Countless columns and books have been written since then, chronicling and making public her private life. Finally, on the heels of a report about a car phone conversation in which a man said he loved her and called her Squidgy, the thirty-one-year-old princess and the forty-two-year-old prince released a statement announcing their formal separation.

True enough, for much of human history, people—and princesses in particular—married very young and for purely practical reasons. And yes, marriages back then seldom ended in divorce. But remember that life spans for both men and women were about half what they are today and that all that was really expected—or permitted—of women was that they keep house and rear children or, depending on their station, that they manage the help and behave like the ladies they were born to be. The question of "personal growth" was never even on the agenda.

Today in this country, however, the actuarial charts put women's average life expectancy at seventy-six, and the huge boomer generation is blooming at mid-life with unprecedented vigor and drive, both physical and psychological, thanks to a lifetime of having basked in the spotlight and a collective belief in the pursuit of everything from fitness to happiness. I have no doubt that this is why women who enter marriage as child brides in the emotional sense very often withdraw from their relationships and go into personal cocoons for further growth. Unless their husbands grow as well, a schism at mid-life or even earlier is all but inevitable. One woman, who emerged from her chrysalis to spread her wings and begin both an affair and a boutique business the minute her third child entered kindergarten, said to me: "My husband is totally bewildered. He senses a change. He keeps saying, 'You're not the girl I married. What happened?'"

The answer, I believe, is that this woman's husband, like many of his fellows, entered marriage expecting the bride to screech to a halt at that point in her development and to remain a girl-woman who would compliantly cater to his needs and ignore her own. The flip side of this is that many women get married expecting their men to change in one way or another. Instead the wife grows up and away from the husband, and he feels angry and abandoned. At the same time she feels angry because he is not developing along with her. In case after case I heard women telling me a version of this scenario—one that I call the Fly Now/Stray Later phenomenon because the women emerge from their cocoons and "fly" as genuine adults, then later form relationships with long-term lovers who meet their newfound needs. The upshot is almost always that the men react by becoming even more demanding, whether in bed or in other areas or both. This, of course, only exacerbates the wives' feelings of being trapped, and many begin to see the men as domineering parent figures. No wonder, then, that these women feel an irresistible urge to turn to their lovers for the respect and mutual satisfaction their emerging selves hunger for.

Even so, the fear of breaking up a marriage, of hurting the children and risking financial instability and community reproval runs strong. That is why an impressive number of the wives I interviewed have stayed in the first marriages and maintained their emotionally fulfilling relationships with their lovers as well. Yet they are not divided selves like the Wife/Wench women we met earlier. On the contrary, the wife who metamorphosizes during her marriage to become a grown-up finds that what she wants is a full and equal relationship. She has in fact become a whole and healthy adult, and she is ready now, as she was not ready earlier, to achieve true intimacy with another adult.

In many cases these women went into marriage with the notion of a union, of the melding of two people into one. In practice, the one person was the man, with the woman as a kind of stunted appendage, Mrs. Him. True intimacy, however, can be achieved only between genuine partners, each with an equal amount of weight to pull. Also, many of the wives in this chapter saw their husbands as saviors. Of course, no one should be invested with a responsibility of that magnitude. Rescue and sacrifice are not what intimacy is all about. An intimate relationship, a good one, is one in which neither party silences, sacrifices, or betrays the self and in which each party expresses strengths and vulnerability, weaknesses and competence in a balanced way.

As Dr. Harriett Lerner points out in *Dance of Intimacy,* intimacy, one of the most basic of human needs, should mean that we can be who we are in a relationship and allow the other person to do the same. It should mean we can talk openly and take a position on where we stand on a variety of emotional issues and allow the other person to do the same. And it should mean, perhaps most important, that we can stay emotionally connected to another person who thinks, feels, and believes differently from us without feeling a need to change, convince, or fix the other person.

The catch, of course, is that one reason many wives end up wanting to fix their husbands is because opposites do very often attract. For example, a person who is emotional and intense tends to select someone who is distant and less emotional. I have long observed that precisely the personality traits which attract one person to another turn out to be negative forces as the years go by. For example, a woman likes a man because he's decisive, but years later she sees him as controlling. Or he likes her because she is willing to give over to him the opportunity to make decisions, but years later he becomes resentful because he feels the whole burden is on his shoulders and he would give anything if she would stop calling the office to ask him about every little thing. Or she likes him because he's very affectionate, but years later she looks at him and finds him smothering and possessive and jealous. Or he likes her because she's very organized, but years later he looks at her as someone who has no spontaneity, who has to plan everything in advance and feels that things have to be just so.

Still, all the wives in this chapter felt a strong need to honor the commitments they had made earlier, when they had not yet evolved. While close to two-thirds of them did eventually get divorced, the rest just didn't have it in them to let go. As one wife said, "What am I supposed to do, just pour his coffee, sit down at the breakfast table, and announce that I'm leaving him for another man? Remember, he hasn't got a clue that I've been having an affair for fifteen of the twenty years we've been married. He'd probably die of shock. Anyway, his only crime is benign neglect. As long as I play the role of the model wife, he just sort of pays no attention to me. So I have a great deal of freedom.

"I know a lot of wives with husbands like mine, but most of the women just get their manicures and get their legs waxed and play tennis. Please, I don't mean to disparage them. They are very good wives and mothers, and they happen to have the luxury to live like that. But I instinctively used my freedom differently. I started taking courses at the local college. I started piano lessons. I dabbled in a lot of things.

"Then I took a seminar on catering, and that was it. That was what I wanted. I had this hidden talent, and unleashing it was the thrill of a lifetime. Pretty soon I was doing parties all over town, and before long I was getting really important clients. This all went on right under my husband's nose, and he'd just say, 'That's nice, dear, whatever you want,' and go back to reading the paper. Eventually I got involved with another man, one of my clients. We had so much in common. But I can't justify leaving my husband for my lover. My husband is a hard worker, and he has given me a safe haven. I was a sapling when we got married, and he provided the environment in which I could grow. The only place I *couldn't* grow was in our relationship. That has been static for all these years.

"But you simply don't destroy a stable family just because your marriage is boring. I have children, and they love their father. They love our traditions. I was thinking about that on Thanksgiving. The kids are teenagers by now, a boy and a girl, and they still like to help me make the pies and so on. They were laughing and talking and teasing each other, and there was that wonderful smell of the turkey roasting. My parents and my husbands' parents and my brother-in-law and his family were due any minute. The table was all set with the good china and silver, and the carving set we got as a wedding present was at my husband's place at the head of the table. All of a sudden I got tears in my eyes, and the kids wanted to know what was wrong. I just said I was so happy. And I *was* happy. But I was sad, too. I'm a lucky woman to have a family like this, and I know that. But I love another man very much. And I'll never be with him on the special day set aside to celebrate and give thanks for our blessings. So I'm a mass of conflicting emotions, and yes, guilt is one of them."

Like this woman, the overwhelming majority of the women in this chapter felt a deep sense of loyalty and appreciation because their marriages had provided the time and security they needed in order to develop fully. Interestingly, most of them report a far greater sense of guilt than do the majority of women who have primarily sexual relationships with their lovers. The sense that I make of this is that while society would like to have women feel guilty about sexual betrayal, many women themselves don't feel that they are doing much more than sharing their own bodies with whomever they choose. On the other hand, while society doesn't condemn wives for having platonic relationships with men other than their husbands, a woman intuitively feels deeply disturbed when she knows in her heart that her marriage is a pretense and her relationship with her lover is a reciprocal and profound love between true soul mates.

As one wife told me, "I started sleeping with my lover after knowing him for about three years, but the sex is just a grace note. It's wonderful, better than sex with my husband, but what I feel guilty about is that I love my lover and I don't love my husband. I don't hate my husband or anything. There's just no feeling, no content. You know something? It just occurred to me that my husband and I never say, 'I love you.' I never thought of that before. My lover and I whisper sweet nothings all the time. I guess the problem is that emotions are so honest and you can't force yourself to feel some way that you don't. Still, I look at my husband, and I think, Poor guy. He's working overtime and handing me the household money, and he doesn't even know that I'm in love with someone else."

Yet no matter how guilty these women feel, they say the need for the lover outweighs the guilt. This speaks volumes to me about the nature of women's relationships. That is, while women are most certainly capable of and deserving of great sexual pleasure, what sustains them in the long run is not the physical but the emotional. As one woman said to me, "Life with my husband is so empty somehow. When we were first married, I was a starry-eyed little bride, just so excited to be Mrs. Somebody and have my own china pattern and decorate our apartment and start saving for a house and a baby. I was twenty years old, and I thought life couldn't be better. I had been dreaming of my wedding ever since I was a little girl. When I was eight, I got a bride doll for Christmas, and she had a little pink trunk with her trousseau in it. My mother had had the doll clothes handmade by a seamstress. This was the most wonderful present, and I was the envy of every girl on my block. We used to play wedding games for hours on end. This was in the fifties, and all we wanted to be when we grew up was a bride and then a homemaker. All of us had junior Betty Crocker cookbooks, too. And when we got to junior high, we joined Future Homemakers of America.

"Now I don't mean to make fun of homemakers. I will be eternally grateful that I was able to stay home with my three boys and bring them up properly. I'm just glad my husband makes a good living and I could stay home.

"I know I'm rambling. What I'm trying to say is that I'm glad I could stay home with my kids, but at the time I never even knew I had a choice. I was totally programmed to fill the roles of wife and mother, and that's that. And my husband was totally programmed to be the man in the gray flannel suit, just commute and work and bring home the paycheck. We were like robots. We never discussed anything. Then, as the kids got older, I got involved with volunteer work, reading to the blind. This really did something to me. First of all, I am not a college graduate, and this was the most reading I had ever done in my life. It opened up worlds for me. And the work was so gratifying. I felt these stirrings of ambition for the first time in my entire life. I tried to talk to my husband about this, about how something was happening inside me, but he just didn't get it. He's a quality control engineer, and he doesn't seem to have—or need—any passion about his work. He just does it. And his reward is a decent life-style. He has his toys: his boat and his car. So I started talking about a different kind of reward, and he just stared at me. He's a wonderful guy. He's always done his share. But he was still a robot, and I was coming to life.

"Then I met another volunteer at one of the planning meetings. This man, in a word, understood. He's ten years younger than I am, but we were soul mates from the start. We started going out for coffee, and then the relationship blossomed. We were together for two years before anything sexual happened, and that was so beautiful and tender, but I still treasure my 'soul food' most of all. I love this man. I don't love my husband. Oh, sure, I *like* my husband. I respect my husband. But I now know that I've never really loved him in the deepest sense of the word. I didn't know that when I got married. I didn't know what love was back then. But I was a different person, a little twenty-year-old with rubber stamp dreams and no mind of her own.

"So would I ever leave my husband? No! I couldn't do that to him or to our boys. That would be heartless. What has he ever done wrong?

He has played by the rules. I'm the one who changed the rules. That's not his fault, and I won't punish him for it."

═══════

This woman is typical of the wives in this chapter. She got married long before she was a fully formed person, and she got married with very pat expectations about her future. While she may have thought she was "in love," she was only in love with the idea of being married, of fitting into the female roles which were strictly prescribed during her childhood in the fifties. Actually, many of the women in this chapter are those who grew up during the era of "I Love Lucy" and "I Like Ike," a decade which has come to be thought of as the norm when in fact it is anomalous in the history of this country. Before that postwar proliferation of GI Bill suburban tract houses, and before the resulting baby boom, women had not been urged toward one "ideal" life scenario but had variously been farm wives, factory workers, professionals, and even Rosie the Riveter types during the war. And while life may have been hard in many ways, most women did have built-in support networks made up of extended families and close-knit groups of neighbors. In contrast, the fifties brought an era of single-family houses and nuclear families—the "American Dream."

Yet for many women the dream was a nightmare. They found themselves prisoners in their own houses, performing endless rote tasks and wondering why they weren't happy when they had everything they had ever thought they wanted. The trouble, of course, was that they didn't have everything *needed*. They had shiny new electric kitchens, washers and dryers, vacuum cleaners, cake mixes, canned soup, and a host of other much-heralded conveniences. They also had husbands who brought home paychecks. And they had children. But they didn't have a sense of self.

Perpetuating this problem, their daughters, the boomers, grew up expecting to be like their mothers. I spoke with many wives who had found themselves in that predicament but who had begun to grow and change as the years went by. Eventually these women happened to meet men who loved them for the adults they had become. At the same time their husbands continued to want only the girls they had married. Most of the wives in this situation expressed a strong desire to leave their husbands for their newfound soul mates, but the majority couldn't bring themselves to do it. "It's amazing what you will sacrifice for your children," one wife said. "I can't justify putting my needs before theirs. I would never break up my family just because I married the first man who asked me and then found out fifteen years later that I should have waited and grown up before I took those lifetime vows."

While the sentiment this woman expressed ran strong, however, a fair number of the wives in this chapter did eventually end their original marriages—not without a great deal of forethought and a full measure of pain and fear—and most of them married their lovers. One woman, who did just that, puts it this way:

===

❥Bev, forty-two: "They say marriages are made in heaven. Well, if that's true, then Jerry and I were meant to be together. We just didn't find each other first. I rushed into my first marriage at the age of twenty-one, right out of college, because we used to joke that a B.A. degree was no good unless it got you your Mrs. degree, too. Jim, my husband, was a handsome playboy type, the quarterback on our school's football team, and I was the homecoming queen. So we were Barbie and Ken, but you can't build a life on something that shallow. I never realized how empty he was until the honeymoon was over and we started Real Life 101. So it's no wonder that when I met Jerry—a man with sensitivity and drive, a man who loved me and listened to my ideas and didn't care that my homecoming queen looks were fading—it's no wonder that I couldn't break up with him and that I ended up leaving the Ken doll for the real man.

"But I hope I don't sound callous. I've been remarried for three years, and there are still times when I have this awful feeling that I owed it to my first husband to have kids and make a go of it. I'll be cleaning a closet and I'll see old photographs of us, and I'll just burst into tears. Or I'll hear 'our song' or run into somebody who knew us when we were the 'perfect couple.' It still hurts.

"People are always citing these statistics about the high rate of divorce in this country, and it makes it sound as though we're all just heartless, that we have no values and that we just discard our relationships like yesterday's newspaper. Well, it's not like that at all. I'm glad I had the courage to move on to a man who is the right husband for me, but I'll never quite get over the fact that I left a man who had never really treated me wrong. Please put that in your book. I am so sick of people wagging their fingers at our generation. The truth is, I don't know of one divorced person who doesn't have some pain and sadness forever."

———

Bev's views are echoed by a substantial number of the women I interviewed, and many women choose to avoid that pain and sadness by staying married and simultaneously living as full a relationship as possible with the lovers who meet the needs of their newly blossomed selves. Casey is an extreme example. She has been married for ten years and is pregnant with her second child. But this child is not her husband's. Her lover of three years is the baby's father, and the pregnancy was most definitely planned.

———

❥Casey, twenty-nine: "I'll never forget the day Rick came into my life. Megan, my daughter, was three years old, and I had just picked her up from her Saturday morning swimming lesson at the Y. We went across to the deli for lunch, and when we walked in, Rick was sitting at one of the little tables, reading the paper. He looked wonderful. He had the most amazing blue eyes. Something just drew me to him, but the attraction wasn't exactly sexual. I can't quite explain it. This is going to sound so corny, but it was almost as though we were looking into each other's souls.

"I kind of shook my head and told myself I had to come to my senses. I knew I had been starved for something lately since my marriage to Phil was just one empty day after another. But you can't just come on to a perfect stranger in the local deli! Certainly not with your little daughter in tow!

"Anyway, Megan and I got our bagels and sat down two tables away from Rick. She was being her usual darling self, saying cute things, and that just broke the ice. Before I knew it, Rick had moved over and was sitting with us. It just kind of happened naturally. I didn't object. We started talking, just small talk, but I suddenly felt as though I had been hit with a lightning bolt. This was what had always been missing from my marriage. Phil and I had gotten married when I was twenty because everybody, including my parents, said he was perfect husband material. And I just kind of went along with it.

"Phil was twenty-five, college-educated, holding down a good job in the personnel department of a big company. He was a gentleman, handsome—the works. And in the beginning that was enough for me. The summer after we were married, we bought a little starter home, and I began nesting, which I absolutely loved. I read cookbooks and made curtains and planted a garden. However, I also worked for three years, and we saved all my money toward starting a family. This was Phil's idea. He is a very organized, very responsible person.

"So at the end of the third year I went off the pill, and I got pregnant four months later. I absolutely loved being pregnant. I never felt sick, and the whole experience was thrilling, almost spiritual for me. The idea that a human being was developing inside me was overwhelming. I took very good care of myself, and Phil was very proud and, in a way, sexier than normal. He liked the whole Lady Madonna thing, too. He liked to see me nude, with my long blond hair over my shoulders and falling onto my breasts. He would run his hands over my belly and feel the baby kick. I almost didn't want the pregnancy to end. I felt like a sacred vessel, someone chosen to perform a miracle. I know people have babies every day, but I'm just telling you how I saw myself then.

"Anyway, I went into labor a week early, and we barely made it to the hospital. The birth was easy, and Phil was right there with me. The doctor cut the cord and handed Megan to her daddy, and Phil handed her to me, and she nestled in and suckled right away. I don't have to tell you we were all laughing and crying at the same time!

"Megan turned out to be such a good baby. She nursed every three hours and slept through the night at eight weeks. I was so happy with my beautiful little girl. After all those years of sitting at a computer terminal, doing data entry, this was paradise. I made friends with some other young mothers, and we would stroll our babies, and chat, and have each other over for lunch. And because Megan was so predictable, I could be sure she would nap just long enough for me to freshen up and have a really nice dinner ready when Phil came home. I got to be quite the gourmet cook.

"After dinner Megan would wake up to nurse one more time, and we'd do bath time and put her to bed. Then Phil would turn on the TV and I would read or do crossword puzzles. We barely ever talked, but I didn't see this as a problem. Everything else was perfect. What was there to talk about? And we made love fairly often. So I had no com plaints.

"Megan grew into the prettiest blond toddler you've ever seen. People would always say that she should be a model. And she was sweet-tempered, not really even a terrible two. She and I had the most wonderful time, going to the park and the zoo. The year she was three, I put her in nursery school two mornings a week and swimming on Saturdays, but I didn't want to overschedule her. I wanted to have every minute with her I could while she was still little. And since Phil and I had been talking about having another baby, I wanted to give Megan a really firm foundation before she had to share me with a sibling.

"Now this brings us right up to that Saturday morning in the deli when I met Rick. We talked and talked and talked—about our families, about the world situation, about everything. It was like a dam breaking or something. I had had all these thoughts for so long. I had tried keeping a journal, and that had been something of a relief, but actually having a conversation with someone—that was incredible. I found myself telling him that I had fantasies of becoming a stand-up comedian since I was always seeing the funny side of stuff, even of bad situations. He really understood that. But he said his big dream, ever since he was a kid, was to become a pilot and see the world.

"Anyway, back to reality. I found out that Rick was married, that he worked for the same company as my husband, and that he had two sons, a three-year-old and a one-year-old. By this time Megan was getting fussy, and I said I had to go. Rick said he had gone out to get some paint at Pergament, and his wife would be wondering what was taking so long. We went up to the cashier, and just before I walked out the door, Rick asked me for my phone number. I felt burning hot, and I almost said no. Then I looked in my purse for a pencil, and I wrote my number on a napkin. I handed Rick the pencil, and he smiled and wrote his number for me. Then he pointed out that the exchange was the same as mine. He said, 'We must be neighbors.' So I told him my address, and it turned out it was only three blocks from his house. I couldn't believe it!

"A week went by, and then I couldn't stand it. I had to talk to Rick. Somehow, just that one lunch with him had made me realize how empty my relationship with Phil really was. One night, before Phil could turn on the tube, I tried to start a conversation, but it never got off the ground. Phil just isn't a deep thinker. He's a nice, decent person, but he'd never know what I was talking about if I said I had some emotional needs that weren't being met. He would just draw a blank.

"So a plan formed in my mind. What would it hurt if Rick and his wife and Phil and I saw each other as couples? That would be innocent enough, and I honestly didn't care whether I ever went to bed with Rick. I just wanted him in my life. Very casually I mentioned to Phil that I had run into a co-worker of his, someone he might have met at the office. I asked him if it would be okay if I invited this friend and his wife and kids over for a barbecue. Phil said sure, and I called Rick the next day. He sounded pleased, and he checked with his wife, and just like that, we were all set for the next Saturday.

"October is still warm and beautiful in Maryland, and we had a perfect day. The children all got along fine, and after they ate their hot dogs, they splashed around in Megan's wading pool while Rick and Marie and Phil and I just chatted about this and that. At one point I mentioned something about how I like to go to flea markets. I think it came up when Marie said she liked a certain vase she had noticed on her way through the living room. Anyway, the phone rang just then and Phil went in to answer it, and Marie got up to go break up a little tiff her boys were having about sharing a toy boat. Rick and I were alone for a minute, and he said softly, 'I'll meet you at a flea market.' I must have looked kind of startled. These are advertised in the local paper, and there are several every weekend, usually starting at the crack of dawn. A lot of people make a habit of cruising around to all of them. You find really good stuff cheap, and it's just a kind of time killer, a hobby. So then I said, 'There are two tomorrow that I know of. Check the paper.' Rick nodded, and then everybody was back and we were all talking again.

"I got up at five o'clock the next day, threw on some jeans and a T-shirt, and headed for the location listed first in the paper. Sure enough, Rick was there waiting for me. He had told Marie the night before that he would be going, and she didn't suspect anything. Plenty of people do this. Well, the market wasn't even set up yet. We parked our cars and just started walking. We ended up in a deserted field, and we sat and talked and talked. After that, we met like that almost every weekend for two years.

"Nothing happened between us sexually. Oh, we kissed and stuff. We cried and held each other. But that was all. We had this terrible sense that we should be together. Still, there was no way we could imagine breaking up two families and disrupting the lives of three little kids who counted on us.

"About this time I went off the pill again because Phil and I had agreed it was time to have another child. The weirdest thing happened. Rick and I were having one of our early-morning talks, and he gave me such a tender kiss, and it suddenly occurred to me that I was fertile again. I wanted Rick's baby. That's all there was to it. I started kissing him really hard, and he almost pulled away, but then he gave in. The dawn was just breaking, and we were on a blanket under a tree. It was a beautiful moment, different from anything I had ever felt with Phil. We lay there for a long time, and then I confessed. I told Rick what a risk we had taken. But he wasn't angry at all. He said quietly, 'Let's make sure you get pregnant with my child. I want us to have a concrete object of our love. No one will ever know.'

"When I got home, I checked my calendar and figured my exact fertile days, give or take a few. Then I was careful not to have sex with Phil during that time, which wasn't hard because he's so easygoing and I'm usually the one who gets things started anyway. It took me two months to get pregnant, and I knew for sure it was Rick's baby. The second month Phil had actually been away on business when I was ovulating, and Rick and I had done it twice on Saturday and once on Sunday, and then again on Monday, when he sneaked over to my house on his lunch hour.

"The baby is due in two months. Just like with Megan, I have loved being pregnant. And now I have two men to marvel over my changing body, my ability to create life! I don't feel guilty. And I'm not worried about what the baby will look like. Phil and Rick are kind of cut out of the same cloth, both about the same height and build and both with brown hair and blue eyes.

"I hope the baby is a boy. A son. Rick's son. Maybe he'll be the one who will go on to be a pilot and see the world. I said that to Rick, and he said, 'Hey, don't be sexist. We could have a daughter who becomes the first commercial airline pilot.' Well, yes, and I suppose Megan could grow up to be anything she wants to be as well. But at the very least I hope she'll wait to get married until she's done a little living, done some growing up. I want her to reach her full potential, whatever that may be. I don't want her to cut herself off and get married just to be safe. Because looking back, I know that's exactly what I did."

━━━━

She's far from alone, of course. As Betty Friedan pointed out in *The Feminine Mystique,* "Girls must be encouraged to go on, to make a life plan. It has been shown that girls with this kind of commitment are less eager to rush into marriage. . . . Most of them marry, of course, but on a much more mature basis. Their marriages then are not an escape but a commitment shared by two people that becomes a part of their commitment to themselves and society." In fact, Friedan's exhortation and the countless subsequent feminist writings it spawned may not have fallen on deaf ears. According to data from the 1980 census, published in *American Women in Transition* by Suzanne Bianchi and Daphne Spain, the age at first marriage for women has steadily risen since the 1960s from 20.3 to 22.8. However, one-quarter of women still marry by the age of 19 or 20, and this has not changed since the early 1960s. And the vast majority of the rest get married before they reach the age of 27. In my own sample, 87 percent were under the age of 24 when they got married, and of those women, almost one-third had gotten married when they were between the ages of 16 and 20. Only five of the wives with secret lives had gotten married for the first time when they were over 30.

Obviously American women still risk making what Thomas Hardy called "the fundamental error of their matrimonial union; that of having based a permanent contract on a temporary feeling." And remember that we have already seen that this "temporary feeling" of being "in love" often masks such other feelings as the urge to escape from a dysfunctional family or the fear of being on one's own. Looking back, one wife said, "It was the spring of my senior year in college, and I was suddenly gripped with terror. What was I going to do? I couldn't go home. I couldn't even stand being home for the holidays. My mother finds fault with everything I do, and my father is a milquetoast who just stands there and lets her get away with it. So you're going to ask why I just didn't get a job and an apartment. Oh, sure. This was 1958, and my parents would have been horrified. What would the neighbors think? I mean, a young lady with her own apartment, or even with a roommate, might have *men* over. So I told my mother I was going to look for a job in New York, which is where I was in school, at Barnard. She said I had to live in a women's residence. I looked at the place. It was like a hotel with these tiny rooms, common bathrooms on each floor, and a dining room where you got two meals a day. There was a lobby for 'entertaining gentlemen callers.' And there was a rulebook with curfews and stuff. You weren't allowed to have a hot plate in your room. You could do laundry only on certain days. No alcohol. No smoking. No 'objectionable behavior.' The place gave me the chills. I'm not a nun. I wanted a rich, full life, with freedom and a family and everything. So I set my sights on a guy in my sociology class, and the day after graduation we got married. We hardly even knew each other. But years later, when I truly fell in love for the first time, I couldn't bring myself to dump the man who had literally saved my life."

True, times have changed in some ways since 1958, but women are still marrying young, many of them getting out of bad families of origin and into loveless marriages. That being so, I would certainly predict that the long-term lover phenomenon will persist as a means of filling the needs of married women when they grow out of their relationships with their husbands.

I would further suggest that Casey is not the only one of her number to have a love child with the lover whom she sees as the man of her destiny. Casey was rather more calculating and forthright than most, but the joke about the redheaded child and the redheaded milk-man is a chestnut that has been around forever. And indeed, a great many of the women with whom I spoke, those who see their lovers as soul mates more than just as a means for sexual release, confessed that they had a definite yearning to bear their lovers' children. Precisely because the extramarital union is not for "recreational sex" but for love in the grander sense of the word, the women—and reportedly the men—want intercourse to have the added thrill of potential procreation. This idea is heightened by the fact that the couples in question feel they are "meant" for each other, even though they met after they had married other people, and so there is an almost mystical urge to know what their progeny would be like.

Yet whether these people actually conspire to have a child or simply take birth control risks—or even when they keep their love child desires at the fantasy level—the two of them definitely connect on a plane beyond mere physical pleasure. Because the women (and often their lovers as well) have become adults *during* the original marriages rather than before, they leave the first spouses behind emotionally and cleave to the lovers who suit their mature selves. The dilemma is obvious. Should they stay in marriages made when they were young and green, or should they break away and marry the men they've been practicing for all along? The women I met made individual choices, depending on just how strong they had become in their own right and how strong the pull toward the lovers really was. Here are some cases in point:

❧**Paulette, thirty-one:** two children, married for ten years to Andy, lover of eight years, John. "I was born in Jamaica, and I came to this country on my own when I was sixteen. I had great dreams of doing something—I don't know what exactly—and becoming rich and famous. My family was wonderful in many ways with lots of love and lots of kids, but we were poor. We did have a TV, though, and it was my dream machine. It put ideas into my head. Anyway, I got myself registered with an agency, and a family on Park Avenue in New York City took me on as a live-in au pair girl, and they agreed to sponsor me for my green card.

"Well! I couldn't believe my good luck. The apartment was an enormous duplex, and I had my own suite. My own bathroom! Back home I had shared a bathroom with my parents and eight brothers and sisters. But what was even better was that the people I worked for were really nice, and the kids were darling—a little boy, ten, and a little girl, eight. All I really had to do was get their breakfast, get them to school, pick them up from school, take them around to various lessons or the zoo or whatever, and give them their supper. Their parents liked to do the bedtime stories, and they all usually went to the country on the weekend. They had a house in Southampton, and sometimes I'd go with them, and other times I'd stay in the city and have my time to myself. I had a nice stipend plus room and board, so I went to Broadway shows and bought pretty clothes.

"Of course, I was a young girl, and the one thing I did miss was having a boyfriend. Specifically I missed Andy, the boy I had been seeing back home in Jamaica. We had started sleeping together when we were fourteen, and we had been inseparable. I wrote to Andy three or four times during my first six months in America and told him all about my wonderful new life, but he never wrote back. I was heartbroken, but I finally made up my mind to forget about Andy and try to meet new people. So you can imagine my surprise when one Friday morning the doorman called up to the apartment to say that a gentleman who said he was a friend of mine was there. He said the gentleman's name was Andy. I almost dropped the intercom! Then I said I would be down to meet him since I didn't want to let anyone into my employers' apartment unless I was sure it was someone I knew.

"It was Andy, all right, just as tall and handsome as ever, with that huge grin and those mischievous eyes. I wanted to throw my arms around him right there, but of course, that wouldn't have been right. He could tell how glad I was to see him, though, and since the kids were already at school, we were free to go out for a cup of coffee and get caught up.

"It turned out that Andy had gotten a position as a live-in gardener/handyman for a couple in Westchester. He had read my letters and decided he wanted to come to America, too. He said he was sorry he hadn't written, but he just wasn't good at it. Now to make a long story short, we started seeing each other regularly, and I got pregnant. We never used any birth control, so what did I expect, but I was young and not too knowledgeable. I just didn't know what to do. By the time I told my employers, I was eighteen weeks along, and so they insisted it was too late for an abortion. They thought I should have the baby, and they'd help me out. They also thought I shouldn't get married unless I was real sure about this boy, since I was only seventeen, so I didn't marry Andy. We did keep seeing each other, though, and needless to say, I was too busy at that point to meet any new boys. Finally, when the baby was four—her name is Chandra—and I had my green card, Andy and I decided to get married. We got a job as a couple—me as the housekeeper/cook and Andy as the gardener/handyman—and we had our own little gatehouse cottage on an estate on the North Shore of Long Island. After two years we had a son, Edward. At that point I was twenty-three years old, and I kind of took stock of my life. I had been lucky in a lot of ways. I felt I had security, a nice life-style, a nice husband, great kids. But I had definitely taken a detour. This wasn't what I had had in mind when I was a little girl, watching TV and dreaming.

"So I started finding time to read. I read everything: Latin poets, Greek tragedies, Shakespeare. And I read stuff by black authors, One, Langston Hughes, really got to me. There were two poems that just struck me in the heart. One was 'Dream Boogie,' and it goes like this: 'Good morning, daddy / Ain't you heard / The boogie-woogie rumble / Of a dream deferred?' The other one was from 'Harlem': 'What happens to a dream deferred? Does it dry up / like a raisin in the sun? . . .'

"I tried to talk to Andy, but he just didn't get it. He's simple and sweet, and I don't think he ever really had a dream. He kind of lives day to day. He works hard, he's a wonderful father, and I should have no complaints. But he just seems to stay the same with every passing year. He never reads; he never wonders about stuff. Eventually I gave up trying to talk to him, but I did ask him if I could take some college courses evenings and weekends, and he really didn't care as long as it was my money.

"I'll never forget the day I registered for freshman comp at C. W. Post University. It was one of those brisk September mornings when there's that scent in the air that just says the world is full of promise. I was on a college campus in America! I was registering for a course! I couldn't believe this was happening. I was a little scared, though. What if I wasn't smart enough? What if everything was over my head?

"Fortunately that wasn't the case. Maybe all my reading had paid off, but I turned out to be a very good writer. After the second essay assignment the professor called me up to his desk after class and told me I had 'remarkable talent.' I almost passed out on the spot. Then he asked me if I would like to submit some poems and essays to the campus literary magazine. He said he'd be glad to go over my work and help me out. I was speechless. Here was this man, the quintessential English professor—square-jawed, leather patches on the elbows of his coat, the whole bit—saying he would take the time to help little me. Finally I mustered the courage to say, 'Thank you, Dr. Whittle,' and I left in a daze.

"That evening I started writing, and after a few weeks, when I thought I had some good material, I submitted it to Dr. Whittle. The next day after class he made an appointment for me to see him in his office at four o'clock that Saturday. He taught the weekend section, which ended at three-thirty. When I got there, he was smoking a pipe and reading my stuff. He asked me to sit down. He smiled and said he wished he had some champagne so he could toast my future. Well, by the end of the year our conferences had turned into dinner dates, and I was calling him John. We had the most wonderful conversations— long, intellectual discussions about literature and philosophy and art. I was in seventh heaven. And it never crossed my mind that I should worry about the fact that he's white and I'm black. After all, we weren't sleeping together or anything. This was strictly a meeting of two minds.

"But when June came, and I realized I wouldn't see him all summer,

I suddenly knew how powerful a connection this meeting of the minds can be. John had opened the door to my soul. He had shown me who I could really be, and he had given me a taste of what it was like to be with a man who is more than just someone to go to bed with. I had changed and grown irrevocably. I could never go back to being my old self.

"The evening of our last class in June was warm and still. The windows were open in the classroom, and the scent of new-mown grass and wildflowers wafted in. I was feeling hopelessly sentimental, and I had to choke back tears as I listened to John's rich, resonant voice and watched him pacing as he lectured, using all the characteristic gestures I had come to love so much: the lift of one eyebrow, the clasping of his hands behind his back, the toss of his head when a stray shock of hair teased his forehead. I couldn't bear the thought that we wouldn't see each other again.

"Apparently neither could he. After class he said in his professor voice, 'May I have a word with you, Mrs. Johnson?' I stepped up to his desk, and he made the pretense of discussing my work with me, but when everyone had left, he said, 'Let's go for a drive.' We each had our own car, and he told me to follow him. We ended up at a beach on Long Island Sound. We took off our shoes and walked along the sand with the gentle waves lapping at our ankles, not saying a word. Once we both bent over to pick up a shell at the same time, and our hands touched. Something wonderful shot through me, a kind of profound warmth, as though I had just drunk a precious elixir. We stood up slowly. His hair shone silver in the moonlight. He pulled me to him, and we kissed for an eternity.

"There was no going back after that. I went home right away that evening so Andy wouldn't worry about where I was, and after that John and I became masters of duplicity, finding all kinds of ingenious ways to meet each other. It's been eight years now, and I can't imagine life without John. Certainly we do sleep together, but you know, it's still that other element that's more important.

"By the way, I have finally gotten my degree, with a major in

English, and now I'm thinking of getting a master's and maybe a Ph.D. I've had several poems and one short story published in 'little magazines,' and I just know there's a novel in me. And John remains incredibly supportive and inspirational. He's my best critic, too.

"So what do I do now? Chandra is fourteen, Edward is eight, and I've been married to dear, sweet Andy for ten years. But I've been seeing John for almost eight years. I don't want to hurt my family, but Andy just isn't growing along with me. I still sleep with him, but I don't feel anything. This is just killing me. I'd like nothing more than to be with John full-time, and since he got divorced four years ago, that would be a possibility. We've talked about it. But would that be good for my kids? I strongly doubt it, and how do you dump a man like Andy who has never done anything wrong in his life? I guess I have no choice but to go on with two men in my life . . ."

For Paulette, clearly a woman of great vision and talent, growing beyond a less complex man was inevitable. Yet like so many other women, she could not bring herself to break up the family she had made a commitment to years earlier, when she was only on the brink of adulthood. She chose the long-term lover solution and made it a permanent life-style. However, some of the women in circumstances like Paulette's did eventually find that the need to be with their lovers outweighed the need to honor early commitments. Even so, these wives did not easily make the decision to divorce. Listen to this woman's voice:

❥Jill, thirty-eight: Two children, married for two years to Mark, former lover for twelve years; divorced two years ago from Lou after fourteen years of marriage. "Let me get right to the point. My husband was selfish and introverted. I never really knew him before we got married since both sets of parents had kind of 'arranged' the match.

They all knew each other socially, and they thought we'd be great together and produce perfect grandchildren. I never really resisted. I had no other plans or ambitions to speak of. I had been an undeclared major until my junior year of college, and then I majored in sociology because it was a gut course. I had no desire to go to grad school. So marrying Lou, who was going to go right into his father's insurance agency after graduation, seemed as good an idea as any. But marriage to Lou turned out to be terminal boredom. He was never mean to me or anything, but he just didn't relate. He read the paper at breakfast, watched TV during dinner, and played golf all weekend. We had sex every Saturday night, like clockwork, and it lasted all of two minutes.

"So life went on, we had two kids, and I became the typical suburban mom. We lived outside Milwaukee, in a nice neighborhood. I will say, my kids—two girls a year apart—absorbed me, and I did play groups, was class mother at the nursery school, the whole bit. But I wondered what would ever happen to me when the nest was empty. I shuddered to think of being alone for years and years with this zombie I had married.

"My solution was to get a part-time job as the receptionist in a dentist's office. I was thinking that if I liked it, I would eventually go to school and become a hygienist. Well, I loved the work. And, you guessed it, I loved the dentist. He was everything my husband wasn't: witty, talkative, full of compliments. We went out for a drink one night after work, and he got into telling me why he loved his work, and I was fascinated. We started seeing each other, and the relationship became sexual after about two years. Then, for ten more years, I stayed married and saw Mark on the side, but emotionally my marriage was already over. And I did go back to school. In fact, I felt some ambition for the first time in my life, and instead of becoming a hygienist, I became a pedodontist, a children's dentist.

"It wasn't hard to keep my relationship with Mark a secret because Lou was oblivious. He could have cared less what I did. So finally, one day, I took my girls out to lunch, and I told them that I was in love with a man I had been seeing for many years and that Daddy and I were probably going to get a divorce. Of course, they were in shock, and they cried and begged me to change my mind. But I was determined. I told Lou the next day that I was leaving him for another man, and he barely said anything. He didn't put up a fight.

"The girls have adjusted very well. They live with Mark and me and see Lou on the weekend. They love Mark now that they've gotten to know him. Which isn't surprising, since he is so wonderful. He has just taken them into his heart, and we have the most wonderful family dinners, laughing and talking about anything and everything.

"As for me, I'm extremely happy. My practice is going well, my girls are turning into lovely young ladies, and Mark is everything I could want. He's proud of me, he's great in bed, he loves to get out and do things—go antiquing or apple picking or go to museums and plays. Anyway, Lou is seeing someone, and I'm thinking that maybe now that he's a little older, maybe he'll make a *choice* of a life partner instead of just taking what he was offered. Maybe he'll be more open with a new wife. Or maybe he'll find someone who likes a nice, quiet guy and doesn't care if her life is unexciting. There are people like that. I have nothing against them. I'm just not one of them, that's all. At least, I'm not now that I've grown up and figured out who I am.

"But I have to add that I still feel some pain and regret that my first marriage didn't last. You know, the mind has a little trick of making bad memories fade and good memories last. It's kind of like the family photo album. You only see the highlights, the good times, birthday parties, beaches, Christmas morning. Everybody's smiling. I mean, whoever says, 'Oh, honey, run and get the camera, the children are fighting again'? So you capture just the good stuff. Well, in the photo album of my mind it's starting to be like that. I remember what was good about my marriage. The bad stuff is fading. And sometimes I wake up crying from a dream about the way we were, so young and planning our future together. I've made my choice, and I'm happy, but I guess you never quite get over a failed marriage."

And so in one way or another Jill and the other women we have met in this chapter grew up during their marriage/lover stage and found personal solutions to accommodate their emerging selves. Those who, like Jill, chose to leave their husbands for their lovers were happy in their new marriages but never completely at peace with having gotten divorced, particularly if they had children. On the other hand, the women who stayed married weren't totally at ease either, since they were more guilt-ridden than any of my other interviewees. There was no ideal denouement to the stories of these women who had made their marriage commitments very early in life, in effect going from financial and emotional dependence in the families of origin to financial and emotional dependence in the marriages. However, another group of women in my sample were already reasonably strong and mature—chronological age notwithstanding—when they got married. They found that marriage put a damper on their personhood, one way or another, and they set out to find an escape valve in the form of a secret love, as we shall see.

4

More Power to Her!

> *Do not put such unlimited power into the hands of the husbands.*
> *Remember all men would be tyrants if they could.*

> —*Abigail Adams*

*T*he Beverly Hills Hotel
takes up fourteen acres on Sunset Boulevard, with the very big and very pink main edifice surrounded by bungalows, swimming pool, cabanas, and tennis courts, all in the *mise en scène* of a variegated tropical forest boasting coconut palms, orange trees, oleander, bougainvillaea, and birds of paradise. Like the movie stars and agents and deal makers who have peopled this legendary lodging place since 1912, the hotel is opulent in the Tinsel Town style that only Hollywood can carry off. I was not at all surprised that Maureen had chosen this as the setting for divulging the details of her secret love. She herself oozes glamour and power. At fifty-five, she is still a head-turning blonde, but she knows enough not to try to appear girlish. Instead she puts herself together so that she looks like the boss lady who definitely wasn't born yesterday.

When she walks into a room, there are invariably whispers of "Who is she?"

The answer, I learned over lunch in a secluded booth in the hotel's fabled Polo Lounge, is that Maureen owns and presides over one of the most prestigious public relations agencies in Southern California, with a stellar client list that is the envy of her lesser competitors.

"And the envy of my husband," Maureen added with a little laugh. "It drives John *crazy* that I'm successful. Never mind that he doesn't do so badly himself. He's a crackerjack entertainment lawyer, and he has a pretty decent client list, but he's always comparing, always competing—always *threatened* by me." She paused while we ordered some Perrier and listened to the waiter's recitation of the day's specials. "The irony of this," she continued, "is that we dated for three years in our early twenties, and that whole time John acted as though he loved smart women and was proud of me. We lived in Manhattan at the time, both of us just out of college, and I must admit, I was a real go-getter. I had spent my entire childhood fantasizing about getting away from my mother. She was the most depressing person, always whining and complaining. My father had died when I was really young—and I was determined to make it on my own. I was never going to be a helpless housewife like my mother. She had taken me with her back to her mother's house after my father died. She didn't even *pretend* to try to get any skills or a job or anything."

The waiter arrived with our glasses of Perrier, and Maureen proposed a toast to women of substance. "So anyway, I thought John was my Mr. Right, but the *minute* we got married, he turned into the epitome of the tyrannical, traditional husband. I couldn't believe it! I swear, we had had a really swell sex life, and all of a sudden he's a prude. And he's saying, 'Isn't that skirt a little too short? And for God's sake, button your blouse. Your cleavage is showing. What will people think?' 'Oh, I don't know, John. Maybe that I'm a normal, lusty woman! Is that a crime?' "

Maureen took a sip of her sparkling water and buttered a piece of her roll. "Things went from bad to worse," she said. "He got transferred to L.A., and I got pregnant. That was 1962, four years before the pill became widely available, and I was using a diaphragm. So I had the baby, and we tried condoms, and, you guessed it, I got pregnant again. So there I was, twenty-six, with a boy and a girl eighteen months apart. And John had turned into some kind of caricature of 'Father Knows Best.' Holy cow! We had a huge fight about my going back to work, and finally he said all right, as long as the job didn't interfere with my 'primary duties.' Well, ex-*cuse* me!"

The waiter arrived to take our orders, and then Maureen picked up the thread of her story. But as she spoke, a new softness crept into her tone. I realized that her brisk and cocky public persona belied the inner sadness of a tenderhearted woman whose marriage had not turned out at all the way she had expected. "To tell the truth," she said, "looking back, I can see that my reaction was pretty dumb. I made up my mind to prove to John that I could handle everything with no problem. In my defense, though, this attitude was fueled by all that stuff we kept hearing about 'having it all,' 'juggling,' that sort of thing. I would like to go on record as saying that having it all means doing it all, which is a totally moronic idea. Right now, you are listening to the confessions of an ex-juggler who wouldn't wish that act on her worst enemy. Up at five A.M. . . . nurse the baby . . . pump some breast milk into a bottle . . . change the baby . . . wake up the two-year-old . . . fix breakfast, and put chicken in the Crockpot for dinner . . . wake up the husband . . . hop in the shower . . . throw on clothes and makeup . . . listen to husband gripe about how long this is taking and when can he stop watching the kids and leave for work . . . kiss husband good-bye, refraining from telling him he's a jerk . . . greet baby-sitter and hand her the screaming baby . . . take the two-year-old to the day-care center so he will have a peer-group experience . . . drive in rush-hour traffic to the office . . ." She paused for breath and grinned. "You get the picture. Definitely not a clambake."

Our food arrived, and between bites Maureen went on to tell me how her husband had become increasingly critical—emotionally abusive, actually—finding fault with everything she did, making fun of her in front of other people, and generally sabotaging her self-esteem. She remembers feeling as though she were drowning, as though she were actually fighting to keep her head above water. That was when her promiscuous period began. A group of her friends took her to a male strip show for her birthday, and she French-kissed one of the dancers and made a date to see him after the show. That was the beginning. For two years after that she hopped from bed to bed, always with a man who was beneath her socially, someone who would really get down and dirty.

"I was on the pill by then," Maureen said. "And the AIDS scare hadn't started. I guess I didn't really think about herpes and other stuff. It certainly didn't stop me. I was like a starving person. Not that this was helping much. In a way I felt emptier than ever."

The sadness that tinged Maureen's voice deepened at this point. "That was a terrible time," she said slowly. "I was going in six directions at once and feeling like a failure everywhere I turned. I'd look at my kids and wonder if I was doing well enough by them. I'd push myself at the office, hoping to get noticed, get ahead, and yet I'd worry all the time that I couldn't compete with the guys who had full-time wives. Then I'd look at John and wonder how things had gone so wrong. And finally I'd sneak off on my lunch hour with some guy I barely knew, have a quickie, and feel good for all of three minutes before the guilt would set in. Awful, just awful."

The waiter cleared away our plates, and we glanced at the dessert menu but settled for just coffee. Maureen's face brightened. "So now we're up to the good part," she said. "I was forty, the kids were in high school, and I had left my job and taken a chance on opening up my own firm. The old drive was coming back, and I wasn't so overwhelmed on the home front. Also, I had gotten really good at just ignoring John. His negative comments sailed right by me. Anyway, within three years I was flying high. I lost weight, colored my hair, got myself an image. I was having the time of my life. So one night I went to a party for one of my clients, and a really impressive, gray-at-the-temples guy started talking to me. He turned out to be a publishing mogul, and we wandered out onto the veranda. It was a perfect starry California night. We sipped our champagne and talked and talked. I told him I was married and had two teenagers. He told me he was divorced and had three teenagers. But I was barely listening. He smelled of expensive musk, and the fragrance mingled with the scent of jasmine in the air. Then he said, 'If there's ever anything I can do for you, let me know,' and I said, 'Well, since you asked, I'd like to go to bed with you.' We left the party and drove to his place. That was ten years ago. Roger and I have been together ever since. He makes me feel worthy and beautiful and sexy all at the same time."

There was a long silence. "There's no need for me to leave my husband," Maureen finally said. "We have our home, our children, our two golden retrievers, our work, our social circle, our routine. We have traditions, the way we celebrate Christmas, the double chocolate cake I always make for his birthday, the once-a-year vacation when we always bring the kids and go someplace special. Why end all of that? Anyway, I wouldn't want to be married to Roger. I mean, I'm afraid that those vows would have the same effect on him as they had on John so many years ago. Marriage is a trap. No, I'll go on just the way I am, thank you very much, with my husband and family for all the world to see, and Roger as my secret." She stopped, smiled, and then said, "My secret strength."

―――――

She's absolutely right about that. Her lover does give her strength. Like the rest of the women in this chapter—about one-sixth of my total sample—Maureen is married to a man whom she sees as bent on breaking her spirit. Her husband's arsenal consists of verbal assaults, and she has found no way to stop these attacks. Yet instead of allowing the insults to weaken her, she has learned to ignore her husband and to listen instead to her lover, the man who validates her and makes her feel good about herself. The lover, in effect, bestows her with the power to go on with her life, in spite of the husband's repeated efforts to diminish her. Ironically, many of the women in this category, like Maureen, are exceptionally bright and talented, and they do have power in the world of work. Typically they achieve great success in the outside world, even as they suffer humiliation in their marriages. The humiliation worsens in direct proportion to their accruing achievements, as their husbands become more and more threatened, envious, and angry that their wives no longer "look up to them." In most cases the husbands' method of destroying their wives' self-esteem is emotional abuse. The need to behave in this cruel and destructive fashion is clearly born of a macho fear of a capable, aggressive woman.

"We met in graduate school," one wife told me. "We were both going for a Ph.D.—mine in anthropology, his in architectural engineering. He always said he admired my 'lively intellect,' and we used to have long, philosophical discussions after we made love, sitting in the dark, propped up on pillows, smoking, and eating. We were in Cambridge—I was at Harvard, and he was at MIT—and the whole setting was so conducive to that sort of thing. I never doubted for a minute that he loved me for who I was, the whole package.

"But then we got married, and there was this weird attitude change on the part of my husband. My dissertation was going much faster than his, and he actually told me one day that it wouldn't be right for me to finish before he did. Then he started sabotaging me, interrupting me for some trivial thing and making me lose my train of thought. He also insisted that I had to type his dissertation since I'm a crack typist and he said we couldn't afford a service. Well, eventually we both finished, but by this time my husband had developed a pattern of putting me down. He loved to do it in front of other people. Let me give you an example. We were at his parents' house—they live in the suburbs of Boston—and his father suggested that the two of us should come to the country club spring fling. It's a formal dinner dance with an orchestra and everything, and I thought it sounded great. So my husband pipes up and says, 'What would Margie wear? She's not exactly a clotheshorse, in case you haven't noticed. I guess you'd have to dress her for me, Mother.' His mother loved that comment, and she is in fact very stylish, so there I was with the three of them laughing at my expense.

Look, we were on a student budget, and OK, I come from a less well-to-do family, and maybe I hadn't developed the greatest taste in the world. But there had to be a better way to handle that situation."

Over and over again in the course of my interviews for this book, I heard variations on that theme. The put-downs were not on the level of character defamation, but they were consistent and insidious, wearing away at the egos of the women subjected to them. One woman said her husband told her she was a terrible driver, and she got so she believed him and let her license lapse. After that he had to drive her everywhere, and he complained and called her a scaredy-cat and a burden on him. Another woman says her husband "teased" her about her laugh, which he called a horse laugh, and she got so intimidated that she stopped laughing in front of people. Almost all the men criticized the wives' cooking and other domestic skills. One woman reports that her husband used to come up to her at a party and yank the cigarette out of her mouth. Not that she doesn't know that smoking is bad for her, but this man would make a public scene, talking about how weak-willed she was. He would do this when he had made sure there were important people present, colleagues of his wife, who is a top-notch casting director.

Not surprisingly the women in these ego-deflating relationships eventually attached themselves to ego-boosting lovers for self-preservation. However, like the women we've met in previous chapters, most of them say they can't bring themselves to file for divorce, in spite of the verbal abuse. Several of these women did mention that they had tried to get their husbands to go for marriage counseling, but most of the men had steadfastly resisted. And the wives of men who did agree to go for counseling report that the husbands spent the sessions reciting laundry lists of complaints about the women, refusing even to consider that they might be culpable in some ways, too. "He doesn't want to change," offered one woman. "He loves hacking away at my self-esteem. It builds him up. He hates himself because he never made vice-president in his company and he's in a kind of dead-end job. So even though he loves the life-style my salary affords us, he can't help being envious of my success. He's so envious he can't see straight! See, I made partner at my law firm a few years ago, so now I make twice as much as he does, and I'll probably make even more as my list of top clients grows. He can't stand that. So he makes mincemeat out of me whenever we're together, both in public and in private.

"What really galls me, though, is that he does it in front of the kids. He'll say, 'Your mother went to Yale, and she can't read an ordinary cookbook.' Now my older son, who's twelve, is starting to team up with him. This is the part that hurts me the most. You know, I was thinking. I always read all the child-care books and articles, and I've tried to do my very best for my children, everything from natural childbirth and breast-feeding on through all the developmental stages. I've given them the educational experiences, the best books and music. I've tried to be there for them. But it never says anywhere in the child-rearing literature what you should do if you and your husband aren't working as a team. My husband undermines all my efforts, and he makes a fool of me in front of my own children. I only hope they'll see the true picture when they get a little older. But in spite of all this, I just can't see getting divorced. Actually, that would probably make things worse. Then my husband would probably get joint custody, and he'd have the kids all to himself on some days. Lord knows what nonsense he'd tell them about me then!"

Certainly, this woman and the others we have just heard from are in nearly insufferable relationships. In spite of all the feminist rhetoric for the last thirty years about the empowering of women, there are clearly many women who cannot break the ties that bind them to controlling men, just as there are many men who fit that description. These men cannot tolerate strong women, and they often use verbal attacks to cut such women down. However, as painful and destructive as verbal abuse can be, some of the women in this chapter have to contend with treatment that is even more destructive and injurious. Some have husbands who are blatant philanderers. Others, though not a large percentage of my study, are physically abused. Also represented here are husbands who drink to excess, do drugs, and otherwise make themselves more and more dependent. There are also "little boy" husbands, those Peter Pan men in search of mothers, not wives. One way or another—whether by an excessive show of emotional muscle or by a display of helplessness or both—these men exert a great deal of control over their wives, keeping them from living their own lives to the fullest. And the women reach for an emotional life raft in the form of lovers who cherish them, who give them the strength to endure, and who make them feel feminine and desirable.

A few of the women, notably those with husbands who are womanizers, say that the initial impetus for an affair was revenge. Yet even these women very quickly moved from this negative motivation to the more positive one of empowerment and self-affirmation. One wife told me: "Yes, my first brief affair was for revenge. But I realized right away that two wrongs don't make a right. There I was, using another person, making love to him when I didn't even love him or know him. I couldn't lead the guy on like that. It was a horrible feeling. I felt sick inside. I ended that affair soon after that, and I vowed I would never do such a thing again. But later I met a man I truly loved. I still love him. We saw each other for a year, and then the relationship became sexual. But I'm not trying to get back at my husband. Not at all. My lover gives me a reason for living. That's not overstating this at all. He infuses me with strength. The lovely thing is, he says I do the same for him. And even though he's very proud of my career success, he also makes me feel *womanly* in a way that my husband never does."

This last aspect of the long-term relationships of successful career women turns out to be particularly important. These high-achieving women are so often seen as "masculine" in this society, and those whose own mothers were homemakers have no role models. They are emotional pioneers, fighting to make it in a man's world and still be appreciated for their feminine nature. For many of them, it is the long-term lovers who help them accomplish that goal. As one woman said, "With my lover, I am totally female. When I know I'm going to be with him, I take special care to wear a sexy bra and panties. All day long, conducting business as the boss of my own advertising agency, I think about the black lace under my tailored suit. But the wonderful thing is that my lover isn't threatened by my business success. He's so proud of me, and he's always asking me questions. But he also brings out the tigress in me. Things get really steamy!"

And so in one way or another all the husbands in this chapter degrade their wives, and most of the wives are particularly powerful women in the marketplace. Interestingly, a majority of the husbands appear to have, in psychological terms, passive-aggressive personalities. The passive-aggressive personality is characterized by a fear of direct confrontation and a narrow emotional range. This leads to an irrational concern about being overpowered and to behavior that amounts to saying yes but doing no. These people have deceptively placid demeanors, and they can't make decisions, even simple ones. They typically do very poorly in personal relationships as well as in the work world. They put things off, they blame others for their errors, and they "forget" to do things requested of them because they see requests as demands. That is why they project onto those around them—particularly their wives—a negative, authoritarian image.

This is the man who says he'll take care of the kids the night his wife has to go to her continuing education class and then calls at the last minute and says he has to work late. This is the guy who says he'll pick up the cleaning on the way home from work because his wife needs a certain suit for an important meeting the next day. But the chore "slips his mind," and the cleaner is closed by the time he gets home.

"This may sound like trivial stuff," said one wife, "but after a while it really gets to you. And the real rub is that my husband makes me feel like I'm a nag and a bitch if I so much as suggest that he's not pulling his weight. So what happens after a while is that you give up. You know you can't count on him, so you stop asking. You do everything yourself, even though you're seething inside."

Hearing this, I couldn't help wondering what had attracted this woman to her husband in the first place. I asked her that, and I also asked countless other women in similar marriages. What is so fascinating is that, as I heard from woman after woman, the passive-aggressive man can be extremely appealing in the early stages of a relationship. He is sweet. He has a good sense of humor, even if there is a little bite to his wit. Also, he appears to be comfortable with a strong woman and will often praise her managerial skills and organizational abilities—aspects of her personality which others may condemn as being too "masculine." At the same time the passive-aggressive man has an irresistible way of "needing" a woman and wanting to please her. He allows her to make the social engagements, choose the movie or the restaurant for the evening, plan the menus, and do the cooking. For a bright and ambitious woman this can be translated as making her feel "feminine." In fact, virtually every woman in this chapter who is married to a passive-aggressive man told me that the courtship behavior of the man had been incredibly seductive in the sense that he constantly praised the woman to others. These men spoke of pride in the women's achievements in the marketplace, but they also rewarded them for such domestic accomplishments as cooking, decorating, and party planning. What's more, for many of these men, sex was not a burning passion since passive-aggressive people often feel uncomfortable with lovemaking. Yet for the women in these relationships, that restraint was a plus. They felt they were with safe, disciplined men who valued them for more than just sex. This affirmed their sense of self-worth, as Kathy makes clear.

"Jerry made me feel as though I were terrific in every sphere," said Kathy, now thirty-eight. "I had been the class nerd in high school, and I didn't even have a date for the prom. My mother was always telling me I'd never get a man because men don't like smart women. So my freshman year in college along came Jerry, and he just started hanging around. He built up my self-esteem, made me feel I was good-looking, and he said he admired my intelligence. Then, one weekend, we went to Traverse City, the cherry capital of Michigan, and we brought home fresh cherries. Jerry lived off campus, and I went to his apartment and baked a cherry pie, and he flipped! He did this darling rendition of the song 'Can she bake a cherry pie, Billy Boy, Billy Boy?' and he said he couldn't *believe* I was smart and pretty and so good in the kitchen besides."

The rest of Kathy's story in a nutshell is that she married Jerry right after college and that they had no sooner tied the knot than what had seemed to be his good qualities turned sour. Where he had once praised her brains, he now felt threatened by her earning power, and he constantly belittled her. And where he once was happy to help with domestic chores, he now became totally resistant to doing anything around the house, saying he was above such menial "woman's work." Not only that, but he began to criticize her looks and her makeup and to tell her she had terrible taste in clothes.

Kathy—who eventually assuaged her pain by forming a relationship with a kind man who became her lover—was one of many hapless victims of what I call the Peacock Syndrome. This is an all-too-common pattern in which men, particularly inadequate men, strut around showing glorious colors during the courtship phase. And women fall for the lure. This answers the often-asked question "Why did she marry a man like that in the first place?" Quite simply he *wasn't* "like that" when she chose to marry him.

Typically, however, soon after the wedding vows are exchanged, such a man shows his *true* colors. During courtship he perceives himself to be in the power position, but when the reality of being married to a woman of many strengths sets in, he begins to feel threatened. That is when he begins his campaign to undermine her self-esteem. And so the question "Why did she stay?" is far more perplexing. Here again, I was struck by the fact that the desire to preserve a marriage is so strong that women will do so almost at all costs. And certainly, once children are born, women will struggle against seemingly insurmountable odds to keep their families intact, even if they are married to men who make life miserable because they see their wives as rivals instead of as partners. One woman said, "I'm well known in my field, and I'm frequently invited to speak for various organizations. They always print a little biography for me, and it ends with the sentence 'She lives in Atlanta with her husband, George, a marketing consultant, and their two children.' George is actually unemployed—or 'between jobs,' as he likes to say. Never mind. I make more than enough for both of us. And our relationship is low-maintenance. He criticizes me, but he makes no emotional demands. That might sound negative, but the plus side is that it leaves me free to concentrate on my kids and my career. Anyway, my point is that I wouldn't know how to take that last sentence off my biography. I don't want to be a failure as a wife. Okay, so my marriage is just for appearances. That sounds so awful, but I know plenty of successful women in the same boat."

Other women pointed out to me that getting a divorce can be extremely expensive and time-consuming. Also, only 15 percent of women are now granted alimony, and in many states women must *pay* alimony if they were the major breadwinners during the marriage. Add to that the so-called deadbeat dad issue, with the vast majority of men failing to pay child support, and many women simply shrug their shoulders and decide that staying married is the lesser of two evils.

Suzanne, a prominent harpist with a symphony orchestra in a midwestern city, is a perfect example: "My husband is a musician also. A violinist. We met one summer at an arts camp when we both were sixteen. I thought I had found the perfect man for me. We dated all through college, and he would send roses when I performed, and he seemed so proud of me. We talked about how we would go to New York and have fabulous careers. We were going to play concertos at Carnegie Hall and get great reviews. At the time we really believed this. We thought anything was possible.

"Then we got married, and he turned into a beast. Just like that. He started criticizing my every move, and he wanted me to give up my music and be the woman behind the man. He wanted me to get a nine-to-five job to support his career. And he refused to get a job. He said it was 'make it or break it time,' and that he had to study and practice. He wouldn't even give lessons. So I got a job as a receptionist. We had to pay the rent after all.

"The truth is, I'm more talented than he is, but we never spoke about that. You could see that he was afraid I would be the one who would get to Carnegie Hall, and he'd never amount to much. He just couldn't handle that. The whole first year we were married, I thought about leaving. But it would have been so complicated. We had known each other for so long, and I had honestly never dated anyone else. We had had a huge wedding, and both families were so supportive. My parents even said they'd give us the down payment for a house. But I didn't want a house. I wanted to go to New York and rent a little studio apartment near Carnegie Hall. However, all of a sudden my husband wouldn't hear of that. He said I was immature, a silly kid with no grip on reality.

"I never left. Eventually I got pregnant. I let my music go for years. I felt as though the real me had died. Then I met my lover. He encouraged me to take up my music again. I was so rusty, and it was a horrible feeling to have lost so much, but I started practicing on the sly, and eventually I got my technique back. My husband was furious, but I didn't care. I got a job with the local symphony. My husband plays a little in a chamber quartet. He still doesn't make a living.

"The thing is, it's just too late to leave this marriage. Actually, a friend of mine in a similar situation did get divorced, but her lover won't leave his wife. And now her kids are a mess. At least my kids *think* we have a happy family. So I leave the illusion alone. Can you understand that?"

———

Yes. Because virtually every woman I interviewed stressed those same sentiments. Preserving the marriage is a priority. Protecting the children is paramount. The lover is to be kept secret no matter what, and he provides not just a sexual outlet but, more important, a source of strength and a feeling of mutual fulfillment and companionship. He becomes the caretaker of her soul. And yet for all his appeal, he is to remain secondary to the marriage relationship, however flawed the latter may be. In fact, even women with physically abusive husbands echo these themes. Let's meet Susan, now thirty-six, a darkly beautiful woman who has been married for eighteen tumultuous years to a man who beats her. She has never told her terrible secret to anyone, not even to her ardent and steady lover of the past five years. But she did at last tell me. Here is Susan's astonishing story:

"My parents owned a flower shop. My brother and I worked in the shop from the time we were little kids, and we actually loved it. We were a close family, and my parents were very strict. We're Catholic, and we went to church every Sunday without fail. I never minded. I was proud of who I was, as I recall, and I remember thinking when I was ten or eleven years old that I believed in the way I was being brought up and that I wanted to amount to something—to make my parents proud of me. I had a dream, as so many little girls do, of becoming a famous movie star. People who came into the shop always told me how pretty I was, and whenever I was home alone, I'd pose and preen in front of the mirror, saying lines I remembered from whatever movie I had last seen.

"So life was basically good. Then, one day when I was sixteen, a man came into the store to get an arrangement for his secretary for Secretary's Day. I guessed that he was in his early thirties—an 'older man' from my vantage point—and he was incredibly handsome, with thick black hair and a wonderful smile. I actually got goose bumps. There was something so attractive about him, and of course, I was also excited by the idea that he was powerful. He had his own secretary, and he just had an air of importance about him.

"Not that he was haughty or anything. In fact, he was so incredibly charming, so nice to little me that I couldn't believe it. He treated me with respect and said he trusted my taste implicitly in picking out the flowers. Honestly, I had never even been on a date at that point. The boys at school all seemed so silly and immature, and I was busy with my homework, my hours at the shop, and my dreams. I had started checking books out of the library on acting and reading the biographies of famous actresses.

"Well, this man and I finished our transaction, and he turned to leave. Then he turned back and said, 'I have my own video production company. We do mostly educational material, but I'm hoping to expand. Give me a call. We might be able to use you in something we have in the works for counseling high school kids about substance abuse. Can you act at all?'

"I nodded, even though I had no idea whether I could act or not. I was speechless. This was too wonderful to be true. He pulled out a business card and left it on the counter. Then he flashed that amazing smile, looking right into my eyes, and he was gone. I stood there frozen for I don't know how long. I felt as though he had been sent to me to make all my dreams come true.

"In my heart, though, I knew I should discuss this with my parents, but I didn't want to. I didn't want them to say no. I didn't even want them to know. This was mine. I had always been the best little girl in the world, and I did love and respect my parents, but the strictness of my upbringing had been starting to get to me. I was a teenager after all. And even though I hadn't really wanted to date, I knew without a doubt that my parents would monitor my every move, give me rules and curfews, and generally keep me on a leash if I did decide I wanted to go out with anyone. They were fairly lenient with my brother, who's two years older, but he's a boy. If you ask me, boys have rights and privileges. Girls have 'shoulds' and 'don'ts.'

"Anyway, I waited two days, and I couldn't get this man out of my mind. The name on the business card was Larry Jones. After that day I couldn't get Larry and his job offer out of my mind. Finally I dialed his number from a pay phone outside the shop. I tried to use my best business voice, and I said to the secretary, 'This is Susan Brown. May I speak with Mr. Jones. He will know what this is in reference to.' I was simultaneously thanking my lucky stars that I had been brought up with business acumen and praying that he would figure out who I was, since even though I had never given him my name, my parents' shop is called Brown's Florist.

"He must have put two and two together because he got right on the line. My heart was pounding so hard I was afraid he might hear it.

But I kept my composure, and we had a very businesslike conversation which ended in making an appointment for the following Thursday at four P.M. This was perfect because I always stayed after school for cheerleading practice until six P.M. on Thursdays, and I figured I would just tell the coach I felt ill and needed to go straight home. No one would be the wiser.

"Let me give you the condensed version of what happened after that. Larry gave me a bit part in the video, but he said he couldn't pay me until I had more experience. He told me I was gorgeous and talented and brainy. He couldn't believe how mature I was for my age, he loved bright women, et cetera, et cetera. He wanted me to go out to dinner, I accepted, and we ended up in bed. I was a virgin, needless to say, and he was actually very gentle about 'teaching' me. I didn't have an orgasm, but I didn't know you were supposed to, so I just thought this was very exciting. I did, however, feel that since I had given him my 'gift,' I absolutely had to marry him. That was my religious training, and I told him as much. He said fine, but we had to wait until I graduated from high school a year from that June.

"So I told my parents, and they went nuts. My mother was sobbing and literally tearing her hair out, and my father was furious. They hadn't even met Larry, but the facts I had given them, especially his age, were enough to cause a scene. My reaction was to withdraw and make up my mind I'd never bring up the subject again but simply elope the minute I graduated. Which is exactly what I did. Larry and I had our blood tests done, got a marriage license, and went to a justice of the peace. Larry's brother and his wife were our witnesses. Then Larry and I went back to his apartment, and I called my parents and told them. This time they didn't make a scene. They were in shock, I think.

"The first month of married life was actually wonderful. I fixed up the apartment, bought some throw pillows and curtains, reorganized the kitchen, bought a bunch of cookbooks, and taught myself how to make wonderful meals. Also, Larry dismissed his secretary and gave me the job, although I wasn't going to get a paycheck. He explained that this was to our advantage, since he would save the secretary's salary, and I wouldn't have to pay taxes, so we'd have more money in the end. That made sense to me, and of course, Larry went on and on about how smart and professional I was and how he was so glad he hadn't married a ditzy woman who wouldn't do her share. I did ask him about more acting opportunities, but he brushed that off and said things would come my way in due time.

"Then, on our one-month anniversary, we decided to celebrate at home. We bought some live lobsters and expensive champagne, and we each had little gifts for one another. We ate by candlelight, with soft music in the background, and I felt so warm and happy. Then I cleared the table and brought out a chocolate mousse for dessert. What followed was so bizarre that I'm going to have to take you through the exact conversation, or else you would never believe a man could give his wife a black eye over absolutely nothing. It went like this:

"Larry: 'Did you make the mousse yourself?'

"Me: 'No. No, I got it at the bakery.'

"Larry: 'I should have known better than to marry an immature little spoiled brat.'

"Me: 'I'm not a spoiled brat! What on earth has that got to do with chocolate mousse anyway? Besides, you yourself have always said how responsible and mature I am!'

"Larry: 'Yes, up until I got close on a day-to-day basis and found out that you have no idea how to run a household. Which is what a woman is *for* after all.'

"Me: 'What? You're the one who was always saying you're glad I'm good at business. Anyway, when would I have time to fiddle with homemade desserts when I work for you a zillion hours a day for no pay? And whatever happened to the part about how I was going to become an actress?'

"Larry: 'Get real! You've got your head in the clouds. You're a married woman, and you are working in a family business. Anyway, no woman is going to talk to me like that!'

"At this point he stood up. I had no idea what was going on. I stood up, too. He started walking toward me, slowly, with his eyes boring into my face. Instinctively I started backing up. That's when he said, 'Don't you ever walk away from me,' and he reached for my arm and yanked me to him. Something popped in my shoulder, but I tried to pull away. He had a grip on my hand like a vise, and he flung me across the room. I smashed into the edge of the china cabinet, catching the corner of it just above my right eye. The pain was instant and intense, but I remember thinking, At least I can still see. Larry didn't say a word. He just went into the living room and turned on the TV. I picked myself up and went into the kitchen. I got a bag of frozen peas and held it against my eye. I poured myself a glass of wine and I turned on the classical music station and I just stood there for a long time. Then I went to bed. I wanted to leave, but where could I go? If I went home, my parents would say, 'I told you so.' And I was too ashamed to tell anyone the truth. I was also afraid to do anything to enrage Larry, now that I knew what he was capable of. Also, I told myself this could never happen again.

"He came to bed after an hour or so. I had been tossing and turning. He reached out, and we had sex. I was afraid to say no. It was absolutely awful. I was relieved when he had his climax. The next morning we didn't say anything. My eye was all swollen, and my shoulder was killing me, but I wore sunglasses to work and told everyone that I had pink eye.

"My shoulder, thank God, was nothing serious, and my eye cleared up within a couple of weeks.

Larry doesn't get violent all that often, but he sure knows how to keep me guessing. I'd say we've had incidents about twice a year, which isn't all that often, but this is no way to live. Still, when I was so young, I couldn't figure out how to leave Larry. For one thing, I hated admitting to my parents that I had made a bad choice. And for another, I only had a high school education, no college, and no real work skills that could get me enough of a salary to live on.

"All that became a moot point, though, because I got pregnant. I was twenty, and we had been married not quite three years. We hadn't been using any birth control, so I don't know how we lasted that long. Still,

I was thrilled about having a baby, and I then had another child right away, so the kids are only twenty months apart—both boys. I adored them from the beginning, but I never got to be a full-time mother, which was a great sadness for me. There was no way Larry could afford to replace me with someone he would have to put on the payroll. In fact, his business had never expanded, and we had even lost some clients. I tried to make excuses, but the truth was, Larry was great at posturing, acting the part of the producer, but he wasn't really all that good at what he did, and he didn't work very hard. My eyes were opened to this pretty quickly, but I had just jumped in to fill the void, covering for him and doing his work to make him look good. Of course, he took all the credit.

"But as I was saying, I couldn't possibly take a leave to stay home with my boys. Fortunately my brother's wife was home with her kids, and we worked out an arrangement where she took my kids during business hours for a fee, so at least the children were with family. I worked like a dog and then went home to do everything around the house. The funny thing was that the better I did, the angrier Larry got with me. Even so, in spite of my best efforts, business started falling off. The recession was partly to blame. So now Larry was furious because I hadn't saved us. He had always liked his wine, but then he started drinking more and more and working less and less. Eventually we folded the business, and I went to work as an executive secretary for the CEO of a big advertising firm. It was a plum position, and considering that I had no real education and had learned everything on my own, I couldn't believe how lucky I was. I made a good salary, I had a nice employee benefits package that covered Larry and the kids, and my boss was brilliant, but a pussycat. He thought I was a prize since I was so efficient and cheerful and his former secretary had apparently been a pain. In the meantime, Larry was sitting at home, being a couch potato. He wasn't even sending out résumés. He would talk about becoming a great filmmaker. He also was doing zero around the house except for messing it up. I would come home after a full day at the office, having picked up the kids at my sister-in-law's house, and find no milk in the refrigerator, laundry heaped in a corner, and Larry watching 'Jeopardy.'

"Don't get me wrong. A proud man who loses his business is a prime candidate for depression, and I know that. But Larry's business was always something of a phony operation, and he was never all that proud to begin with. I say this with the wisdom of hindsight. And you're still wondering why I didn't leave him, right? Well, he may not be proud, but *I* certainly am. I was going to make a go of it come hell or high water. I was *never* going to admit to my parents that I had made a mistake, and I made up my mind to get Larry to go with me to a marriage counselor and maybe to AA. Remember, I'm also very religious, and I just couldn't handle the idea of a divorce.

"Getting Larry to go for counseling was impossible, however. He's just too stubborn and macho. The whole thing was really getting to me, and I started getting sick. Nothing big deal, just one cold after another and various aches and pains in my neck and shoulders. I tried never to miss a day of work, because I couldn't afford to lose my job, but once when I had the flu with a hundred-and-three-degree fever, I simply couldn't drag myself out of bed. My boss was very sympathetic, and he called twice that day to see how I was. We ended up chatting for quite a while, just aimless talk about the weather and so on. But we had never done that at the office. It was always 'Mr. Carlton' and 'Mrs. Jones,' very formal.

"Well, the next day, while I was still out sick, he phoned again, and he called me 'Susan.' Lying in bed all feverish that afternoon, I kept hearing Mr. Carlton saying my name over and over in my head. I started fantasizing about ways to leave Larry without getting hurt. And I fantasized about Mr. Carlton. His first name is Christopher, and in my mind I started calling him Chris. Once, when I was kind of half asleep, I actually had an orgasm, just dreaming about making love to Chris. I was already the mother of two children, and that was the first orgasm I had ever had in my life. I had done it all with my mind. I hadn't even touched myself. I was overwhelmed! It was fantastic, and I wanted so much to know what it would be really like to make love to Chris.

"The next day he called again, and I realized that just his voice could turn me on—so mellow, so kind, so sexy. And that afternoon a dozen red roses arrived for me. Larry didn't think a thing of it since this guy was my boss and we had always been on formal terms.

"Well, when I got back to the office, still a little sick with a cough and sniffles, Chris was so solicitous and sweet. That's when we got on a first-name basis. And it wasn't long after that before we were seeing each other. The logistics weren't so hard, since Larry was in a fog half the time and I would just have my sister-in-law keep the kids overnight. I'd say I had to work late. It's been five years now, and Chris is the most wonderful thing that ever happened to me. He makes me feel beautiful. The sex is fabulous. And the best part is that he makes me feel special, like nobody could ever take my place.

"Of course, nothing can ever come of this, since Chris is ten years older than I am, married, and the father of three boys. But I'll take what I can get. Chris makes my life worth living. Oh, by the way, he has asked about the occasional bruises and so on, but I just tell him I'm clumsy and I walked into the furniture or something. He's never pressed me beyond that.

"Sometimes I still try to scheme and figure out how I could leave Larry. Maybe when the kids are older, I will. But right now I can't formulate a plan that I'm sure would work. Once I told him I was leaving, and instead of getting abusive, he started crying like a baby, asking me how I could do that when he needs me so much. Actually, I am concerned about that. He'd probably end up dead on the street. He drinks a lot now and seems to have no ambition at all. I'm a compassionate person, a religious person. I'm the type who would take in every stray cat if I could. So how can I turn my children's father out when he's not capable of taking care of himself at this point?

"The other thing is that I'm afraid to leave him. As I said, the one time that I broached the subject, he got all weepy and pleading. But I wonder how he would react if I really did get up the nerve to file for a divorce. I have nightmares about that. I also have nightmares that he'll find out about Chris and do something terrible. This is a big risk I'm taking, seeing Chris. But we've managed to keep things a secret, and I trust we always will.

"Anyway, the risk is worth it. Chris makes my life bearable. He's my secret treasure, something to look forward to when times are tough. When we're together, laughing and making love, life is precious and perfect. I save those moments in my mind and play them back when I need them. I'll never give up my relationship with Chris as long as I live."

=====

If Susan's story affected you as much as it did me, you can't help feeling great compassion for her. As a psychologist I felt a strong desire to help this lovely woman, to show her that she is what has come to be called a codependent—a person so attuned to the needs of others that she will rush in to rescue the most thankless of people at her own expense. Of course, Gloria Steinem says that this is what all girls in our society are brought up to be. Still, we should remember that Susan had resisted the message early on. She was once a delightfully headstrong young girl with dreams and grit. But as such she was a prime candidate for the wiles of an emotional impostor, and she found herself trapped at an early age by a man who had led her to believe he was not only strong in his own right but her biggest booster as well. In truth, he was weak and manipulative, using scare tactics as well as brute strength to make sure that she was kept in her place and that she also continued to take care of his needs. Susan thought she was falling into Larry's arms, but in fact, she fell into his hands and became his pawn. The first clue was when he refused to pay her for working in his business, yet while that seems obvious in the retelling, most of us find it difficult to be wary and vigilant in a relationship simply because the sensation of being in love inspires unalloyed trust in the other person.

Obviously that can be dangerous. Yet I must admit, having heard Susan's story told from the heart, I did understand why she couldn't figure out how to leave him. In part she was too compassionate to leave him with no resources and no support. But in great measure she was afraid of what might happen. In fact, her fears are not unfounded. Dr. Samuel G. Klagsbrun, who treated Hedda Nussbaum, the abused companion of Joel Steinberg, the New York lawyer jailed for lethal child abuse, contends that such women find a means of survival that is similar to that of prisoners of war or hostages. They try to behave properly, to accommodate their captors, and to get through each day hour by hour. As one woman put it, "I'm just constantly trying not to ruffle his feathers. The problem is, you never really know what's going to set him off. But I realize that I have a special tone of voice that will calm him down. I become very sweet, very gentle. I compliment him. I tell him what he wants to hear. And I always agree with him when he criticizes me, and I apologize and tell him I will try to improve. He loves that, absolutely loves it. Because then he has 'won.' Of course, I hate doing this to myself. I hate living like this. But I'm trapped. I can't imagine how I would escape."

Actually, escaping turns out to be nearly impossible for women like this. Sarah Buel, once a battered wife and now a Harvard Law School graduate who is an assistant attorney for Norfolk County, Massachusetts, says that the problems abused women face when they want to leave are: (1) not enough money, (2) finding a place to live for themselves and their children, (3) fear of losing their children if the men control the money, and (4) fear of more violence. This last fear is very real since statistically more women are killed when they try to leave than at any other time. Leaving must be carefully planned, and a woman needs to enlist the protection of friends or social workers.

And so Susan didn't risk leaving. She turned instead to a lover to soothe her pain and give her good times to look forward to and good times to remember. Similarly, other women in marriages not quite as grisly, but equally oppressive in one way or another, have found lovers who ease the agony. Many of them are women with husbands who are womanizers. "This is the ultimate put-down," one wife said. "Your husband is supposed to make you feel special, beloved, like you're his one and only. Then it turns out that he could care less. He leaves you at home, doing the dishes, and he goes out with other women. My husband makes a good salary, and so he treats himself to call girls. I saw his American Express bill, and there were charges to an escort service. This makes me feel like a little nothing. A nobody. I'm his domestic servant, but I'm not desirable, not sexually and not emotionally.

"Then, when I was forty-five, I found a man who is true to me. He has built me back up. I feel like a woman and a person again. I feel strong and powerful. It's so wonderful. But my lover is married, and they have four kids. He'll never leave his wife, and I know that. So we go on the way we are. One time I tried to figure out how we both could get divorced, but just the practical stuff like medical insurance blew me away. I gave up the idea. It's too complicated."

This woman, like many others in similar situations with whom I spoke, was so weakened by her husband's obvious philandering that she never even thought of getting back at him, and not until she chanced to meet a man who loved her did she even entertain the idea of having an affair. However, some women with husbands who fool around do decide to get revenge. As we have seen, however, this is a negative reaction that ends up being emotionally draining rather than empowering. Consequently, the women I spoke with all put an end to the revenge phase and eventually wound up with long-term lovers who gave them strength. Here is one of those stories:

―――

❯**Lorna, forty-four:** Two sons in college, married for twenty-four years to Frank, lover of seven years, Tim. "I was a faithful wife for seventeen years, all the time I was bringing up our boys. Frank was a womanizer from the start. This was a total shock since he had told me I was his one and only while we were engaged. And he didn't even bother to shield me from this behavior. I think he loved the idea that he could make me feel so lousy.

"He is a contractor—very successful financially—and his office has always been in our finished basement. He has his own phone line. I would be in the kitchen, making dinner, and I would hear his conversations floating up the stairs. He wasn't doing business, believe me. He'd be talking all dirty and sexy to some woman.

"Yes, I confronted him on several occasions, but he just shrugged me off and said I was a raving lunatic. What was I supposed to do? I was home with two little kids, and he was making all the money. I was trapped. So finally, when the kids were in high school and I was thirty-seven years old, I got into volunteer work at the hospital. I was a candy striper, and I loved it. It got me out of the house, and I felt so useful, making sick people feel better. But then Frank, my husband, started having a really all-out affair with a certain woman, and I knew he was even paying for her apartment. Believe it or not, she went to our church, and I would see her there and want to throw up. So I got really depressed, and one day at the hospital, when I was on my break, I went into the lounge for some coffee, and this young intern, Tim, sat down next to me. We had been friendly for a while because our schedules usually coincided. He was just darling, and we would talk about anything and nothing. On that particular day I must have looked really glum because he said, 'Hey, let's get out of this place and go across the street to the coffee shop for a little change of scene.' We had done this before, and seriously it did help to get out of that hospital atmosphere for a little bit.

"We ordered our coffee and a muffin, and Tim was trying to get a conversation going, but I was not very chatty. My mind was all tangled around Frank and his mistress. I couldn't stop thinking about how he had been cheating on me for the whole seventeen years of our marriage. For some reason, it was just boiling up inside me, and I was getting more and more furious. So then Tim said, 'Hey, what's the matter? I can tell something's wrong. Is there anything I can do for you?'

"I looked right at him and said, 'Yes. I want to make love to you.' He grinned and signaled the waitress and said, 'Check, please.'

"We went to his place since he's a bachelor, and I'll admit that the first time was for revenge. But after that I wouldn't say so. Tim became my secret, and there is a certain sense of power in having a secret, but it developed into more than that. I stayed with Frank because of the kids and the money, period. That was it. Everything else was just going through the motions. My real life, my real feelings were with Tim.

"They still are. He's got a girlfriend now, and I'm jealous of her, but what could I expect? He's young, and he's going to want to have a life. I suppose if I could get up the nerve to leave Frank, Tim might marry me, but I'm not going to risk that. What if Tim suddenly didn't want me? Or worse yet, what if we got married and Tim turned into a version of Frank? I mean, right now he's sleeping with me and with his girl-friend, so he's not the faithful type. But then neither am I. So I'll just go on the way I am. It's not so bad."

Here again the long-term lover solution has served as a form of psycho-logical salvation. While Lorna's first assignation with Tim was out of revenge—one of the classic reasons women have always given for extramarital liaisons—she quickly moved into a more profound rela-tionship with him and became sexually faithful to him, except that she continued to accommodate her husband by sleeping with him also. And like the other women in this chapter, she found that the affair actually helped her marriage in that it gave her the strength to stay with a husband who is behaving in an intolerable fashion. There were several similar cases in my sample, but one stands out. Jeannette, now thirty-nine and married for nineteen years, initially made a very conscious decision to go out and get what she wanted:

"Kenny and I were both virgins when we were married. We were these two sweet kids who planned a perfect wedding, got all the perfect gifts from the bridal registry, bought a cute little house, and looked forward to a simple, ordinary life, married with children. We promised we'd be forever faithful. I thought we had undying love. At least that's the version Kenny led me to believe *before* we got married. But it didn't take him a year before he was having one-night stands. I swear, he would leave clues so obvious that any idiot could have figured out what was going on. I thought about leaving him then, before we had kids, but wouldn't you know, I got pregnant. We'd been using foam. I guess I should have known better. Oh, well. I did want kids, and I talked myself into believing that fatherhood would make Kenny get serious and settle down.

"Ha! If anything, he got worse. He's a salesman for a computer company, and he started traveling quite a bit, and I knew what was going on in those fancy hotels. By this time I didn't want to leave. I wanted to get even. Why should I get a divorce when my daughter was so little? I could stay, live in my nice house on Kenny's money, take care of my daughter, and have some fun of my own. So I had my tubes tied, and then I put an ad in the paper. It said: 'Nice married lady looking for sex with no commitments.' I rented a post office box so Kenny wouldn't know what was going on. I got over six hundred responses, mostly from married men. I separated them into three piles: yes, no, and maybe. A hundred made it to the yes pile. I went out with forty of them in a span of eighteen months and slept with thirty of them. They were lawyers, stockbrokers, engineers, architects. This was before AIDS, or I'd probably be dead by now.

"Did I have a good time? Not really. I just liked the idea that I was desirable, that no one ever turned me down, and that I wasn't letting Kenny get away with some double standard.

"About that time I saw a personals ad from a man that said, 'Single white male looking for more than sex.' I was intrigued. I answered, and Matt called me. He's five years younger than I am, well educated, from a wealthy family, and very cultured. I was awed by him. He genuinely liked me, and we dated for a whole year before we slept together. We went to plays, the opera, the ballet, fine restaurants. He gave me a whole education. He made me a better person. I adored him. And when we did sleep together, it was tender and beautiful, an expression of our love.

"Our relationship has gone on for years like that. I hope it goes on forever. Sometimes I think back to when Kenny and I were young and engaged. Kenny really tricked me. He wasn't what he said he was at all.

But I'm older and wiser, and now I've got a wonderful, honest man. Better late than never."

＝＝＝＝

Here a woman who had initially behaved in a very independent and calculating manner in order to seek revenge had eventually grown past that phase and found real power in the form of a sustained affair with a good man. As Jeannette herself said, "Revenge is dark and evil. I didn't get any real pleasure out of being vindictive. And I felt bad about using men like that. With my lover it's different. We are together because we want to be together. We care about each other. This is not about revenge at all. The truth is that I would love to marry my lover. But I don't want my daughter to come from a broken home. I just can't do that to her. Kenny may be rotten to me, but he's super with her. And he makes a good living. We'll be able to send her to a good college. She's a bright kid, and I want her to have every opportunity, every advantage. That's why I stay married."

＝＝＝＝

There's that familiar refrain again. We've heard from three groups of women: those whose husbands fail to ignite them sexually, those whose husbands don't give them a sense of companionship, and those whose husbands are in some way cruel, abusive, and resentful. Yet all the wives insist that they feel an overwhelming need to preserve their marriages. Some do so out of loyalty, some out of financial need, some out of pride, some out of a combination of these factors. But all the women who are mothers—more than 80 percent of the sample—said they would go to any lengths to give their children financial and emotional stability. That is why, even though the affairs are so important to these women, they also said they would end their affairs if those relationships ever threatened to jeopardize their marriages. This is precisely why the wives are so scrupulous about maintaining secrecy.

In that regard one wife told me: "You would be amazed at how easy it is to pull this off if you are careful. My lover is a very courteous, thoughtful man, and he doesn't want to hurt his wife and kids any more than I want to hurt my husband and children. From the very beginning we have had our guidelines: No phone calls at home under any circumstances; always respect family obligations and place them before the relationship; respect time limits in terms of what time you said you'd be home; never put down your spouse or the other person's spouse. We never break these rules.

"We've been together for seventeen years, and this is the most comforting, beautiful relationship. I'm myself with this man in a way that I have never been with anyone. Think about that for a minute. People, women especially, are always trying to conform to other people's expectations. I was the quintessential good little girl in school, striving to please my teachers and my parents. I was trying to be who they wanted me to be, without ever asking who *I* wanted to be. And then I tried to please my high school boyfriends. I tried to please my first boss and my co-workers. I would rehearse sentences in my head, so I could say the 'right' thing. I was afraid to disagree, afraid to voice an opinion for fear of making a mistake and being ostracized or ridiculed. Then I married a man who took complete advantage of my desire to please. He has bullied me and belittled me from the day we got married. I was so frustrated at first because all I wanted was his acceptance, but I could never do anything right.

"Finally, I found my wonderful lover, and something in me just knew that it was okay to relax, to say what was on my mind. It was okay to make a mistake or disagree. I didn't have to be perfect. This was such a relief. In bed and out of bed. It's a miracle. But I've been married for twenty-four years, and I'm going to celebrate my silver anniversary in style. I'm going to stay married. That's why my lover and I are so careful to keep our relationship our own wonderful secret."

Keeping their lovers a secret was a priority for all my subjects, of course, but the women we will meet in the following chapter were not as successful as those we've already met. The reason lies in the fact that all of the next group of wives suffered more blatant forms of abuse, neglect, or abandonment as children than did the other women I interviewed. Consequently, they entered adulthood with a paucity of interpersonal skills and an inability to form intimate relationships. Let's find out how the long-term lover life-style works—or doesn't work—for them.

5

Nobody's Baby

There is no disguise which can for long conceal love where it exists or simulate it where it does not.

—La Rochefoucauld

*P*icture the front porch of a rambling Kentucky home, complete with a swing and redolent of magnolia blossoms. Lily had described the place she grew up in so clearly that I felt as though I had been there. Even sitting across from me in a restaurant in Cleveland, Lily remained every inch the southern belle—a true Scarlett O'Hara look-alike with a seductive drawl and come-hither posture, politely tempered by the unmistakable patina of good breeding.

"I went home for two weeks last summer, just the way I always do," Lily said, with a mischievous smile and a wink. "My daddy thinks I'm being a good little girl, finding time to visit with my family. But the truth is that I wouldn't ever go back to Kentucky just to see my family. My daddy has been pushing and criticizing me since the day I was born. I couldn't wait to get out of that house. I tried to please him when I was younger, but I've given up. It's useless." She paused; then her frown gave way to a wonderful, breathy laugh. "See, the real reason I go back to Kentucky is to see Billy Bob. He's been my boyfriend since I was seventeen and he was thirteen. Like they say, you never forget the first time. Well, actually, it was *his* first time, and my first time with *him*, if you see what I mean," she continued. "We had been swimming, and we were getting some sun by the riverbank. I thought he was the cutest little thing I'd ever seen. I started flirting and being real sweet, and we ended up in the backseat of my car. You could say I taught Billy Bob everything he knows. But he was a real quick study, believe you me.

"So we had our wonderful romance, and then I graduated from high school and went off to college in Ohio—Oberlin, because my father said it was the best place for music. I had studied the piano all my life, and he was the one who made me practice. I was an only child, and he once said I had to be both a son and a daughter to him. He would actually crack me across the knuckles with a ruler if I missed a note. He had always wanted to be a musician himself, but his parents were against it, so he was always telling me how he was giving me the opportunities he had never had. When I was a little girl, it struck me funny that he never stopped to ask whether I *wanted* the opportunities or not. But I showed some talent, so I just went along with what he wanted.

"Not that I could ever please him, as I said before. He would come to my recitals, and afterward people would come up and tell me how well I had played, and he would find some fault: I hadn't played the crescendo with enough power or whatever. For years I was crestfallen over this, and I'd make up my mind I was going to get so good he'd *have* to approve. Through all this my mother was just kind of there. She was a beautiful woman, and she tried to be the perfect wife, but my father never gave her any strokes either. He always managed to find fault with her. Then, in the afternoon, they'd have their martinis, so the anger between them would dissipate by suppertime.

"My mother died of breast cancer when I was in my junior year of college. I had a mastectomy myself two years ago. I think I'm cured, but you never know. I'm forty-six, just the age she was when she died. So young! But I don't think about it. I've made up my mind to live, live, live until I die. I give piano lessons, and I also play for a ballet school, which I absolutely love. And I have a wonderful circle of friends. I'm lucky enough to have a small trust fund from my daddy, so I don't worry about money. I can travel, do whatever I please.

"I'm married, and I have been for twenty years, but my husband and I have had separate apartments for the last ten years. Jerry and I are on good terms, but I just can't take being around someone twenty-four hours a day. I'm a loner. Maybe it was all those years of sitting by myself, practicing the piano. Anyway, Jerry and I go out, and we take lovely vacations together. I suppose he sees other women, but that's his business.

"I don't have any children, so I'm free as a bird, which suits me fine. I don't have to answer to anybody. But what I really wanted to tell you is that Billy Bob has always been a part of my life. It's the best little no-strings-attached arrangement you can imagine. Every time I see him, I feel as young as when we spent those lazy summers by the river. He's a constant, somebody I can always count on to be sexy and fun, but I don't have to prove anything to him. It was always like that. I remember how I loved the feeling right from the beginning that Billy Bob was my little secret and my daddy would never know. He still doesn't. My husband doesn't either. And Billy Bob's wife and little boys don't know. He's been married for fifteen years and has three sons. They call me Aunt Lily, and I bring them heaps of presents. They are just as darling as their daddy, and I love youngsters as long as they're not mine.

"So there you have it. Not a bad life. A little different from most, I suppose, but I'm happy. How many people can honestly say that?"

I kept in touch with Lily. The cancer reappeared in her lungs. She died within a year. At her request the coffin was closed. On a table nearby was a photograph of Lily in her prime: beautiful, flamboyant, with that radiant, saucy smile. Lily's husband and her lover each stopped for a long time in front of her photo. They smiled, each one with his private memory of the funny, vibrant, willful woman Lily had been.

There was, however, one man who didn't smile as he looked at the photograph. Lily's father. I watched as he stood there, his arms folded across his chest, his face expressionless. He and his daughter had never really made their peace. Yet I found myself doubting that they would have even if Lily had lived. After all, I had spoken with many, many women in my sample who continue to this day to wrestle with situations similar to Lily's. To all onlookers, Lily's family of origin was a model one until her mother's untimely death. Her father and mother had an ongoing marriage, they were at least ostensibly faithful to each other, and the father was a good provider while the mother was a good homemaker. As an only child in this affluent family Lily was lavished not only with material things but with education and opportunities for travel, plus cultural experiences. Even after her mother died, she received her father's continued support in the sense that he had a trust fund for her, and he always welcomed her into her childhood home whenever she wanted to visit. Certainly, given the horror of some children's lives—and we will hear about some of them as this chapter progresses—Lily was a privileged youngster. She herself was quick to acknowledge that. But the human spirit does not live by bread alone. And Lily's spirit was never really nourished. Her father, in the name of love, was a critical, domineering, and self-serving man who held out his affections as a possible reward for Lily's accomplishments. But he always snatched the reward away just as she thought she was about to obtain it. From this Lily and others in her situation learn that love is not freely given and is not unconditional. They learn that love must be earned or won and that earning or winning it is nearly impossible to do. In effect, they learn that they are not worthy of love. Beyond that, they learn that the love they have to give is worthless also, since the punitive and manipulative parent never truly accepts the gift of the child's love. For a female, after all, the father is the first male she loves and the first male she hopes will love her. If this relationship never gives her the affirmation she needs in order to grow into a woman who believes she is both deserving of love and capable of giving love, the odds are great that her ability to form healthy attachments in her adult life will be seriously impaired.

In Lily's case, as in many others, the problem was compounded by the fact that the mother was a kind of emotional nonentity. In other words, there was no strong female role model and no chance to learn how to love and give love with the mother any more than with the father, albeit for different reasons. The mother is sometimes simply a self-centered person with no real interest in the child. More often, however, the mother is a person with low self-esteem who is cowed by her domineering husband and is determined to keep the peace at all costs—a pattern, incidentally, that we have seen in the lives of many of the women in the previous chapters. The daughter of such a mother does not see the mother stand up to her husband and ask to have her needs met. Nor does the child see her father ever put his own needs aside to please his partner. She grows up not knowing that such a scenario is even possible. The cost, in most cases, is the loss of the child's sense of self-esteem and of her ability to form healthy love relationships later in life. I am convinced that for women like Lily, difficulty with genuine attachments in adult relationships stems from the early, skewed lessons in love which they learn in their families of origin.

However, what is so fascinating is that even for these women with impaired "love mechanisms," the need to hold their own marriages together in some fashion is extremely strong. Considering the fact that the divorce rate has tripled in this country during the last thirty years, and now stands at about 55 percent, the determination of all the women in my sample to *preserve* their marriages is remarkable. Lily's solution—staying married but maintaining separate apartments and a lover—is a bit unusual, but it worked because she had no children and because her husband apparently liked the freedom as much as she did. Still, the two of them were very serious about maintaining their marriage, and Lily once proudly showed me her photo album, from the wedding day on. She and her husband, maturing over the years, appear in photo after photo, variously blowing out birthday candles, opening Christmas presents beside a beautiful tree, and vacationing in the Caribbean. Looking at the snapshots, one would have no way of knowing that this couple barely saw each other in between the photo opportunities and that the wife, at least, was leading a secret life with a lover she had known for years, even longer than she had known the husband.

Actually, for many other couples in this chapter who continue to share homes but not their hearts with their husbands, the situation is really not so different from Lily's. The women spend their lives under the same roof with their husbands, but the relationship is pretty much devoid of content. As one wife said, "The truth is, I'm not really in love with either my husband or my lover. I sleep with both of them, and I enjoy more of a friendship with my lover than with my husband, but I'm not passionately involved with either one of them. Frankly, I get more excited about my work than I do about my relationships. I own a restaurant and we got a Michelin Five Star rating last year. That was my finest hour. See, I'm the chef also. Not many female chefs have done what I've done. And I didn't even start seriously until my kids were in high school. I went to Paris and took a Cordon Bleu course, and that was the beginning of fulfilling a lifelong dream. It's a tremendous amount of work, but it lights my fire.

"Sometimes I think it would be easier if I didn't have either man in my life. They take a lot of my time and energy. But then I think about my children, and maybe pretty soon my grandchildren, and I can't imagine destroying our family. My husband is a nice guy. My lover is a nice guy. And as I said, of the two men, my lover gives me a lot more in the way of friendship. So I'd be crazy to end that relationship, wouldn't I?"

This woman, like Lily and all the women in this chapter, has much less intense relationships with the men in her life than do the women we have met in previous chapters. And like the majority of women in this chapter, she has found a passion for something besides people, and this ardor sustains her in a way that love relationships sustain some other women. All that notwithstanding, however, for the women in this chapter, the ideal of maintaining the marriage is still the overwhelmingly prevalent sentiment in spite of the fact that these are women with no real role models for a healthy marriage and family and no real ability to make a commitment to loving one man and to accepting his love.

"Nobody wants to get divorced," one wife told me. "Ask any bride on her wedding day what she thinks the future holds, and you can bet she's not going to say, 'Oh, I'll probably get divorced after a while.' I mean, hope springs eternal. Every couple that gets married figures that they're going to do it right. They're going to be successful. I think especially if your parents had a lousy marriage, you get kind of uppity, and you figure you can do better. I know that's what I thought. My mother was a witch with a capital *B,* and my father was this cringing little henpecked guy. There was always tension, always nagging. I made up my mind to get out of there the minute I finished high school. I wanted to have a career and marry a man I could respect. I pictured us as equals in the relationship. But whatever I did, I wasn't going to end up like my parents."

Like this woman, a substantial number of the women in this chapter had harsh, critical, unaccepting mothers and passive, uninvolved fathers. This is the flip side of the scenario we saw with Lily, who had a punitive father and a passive mother. Many women in the group with critical mothers and weak fathers had mothers who were traditional homemakers. These mothers were clearly threatened by and angry at their daughters' attempts to have careers. True, some of the mothers did work, but they had traditional female jobs—for example, they were schoolteachers or hairdressers—and they were upset at their daughters' dreams of making it in a man's world, perhaps as a lawyer, an M.B.A., or a physician. Also, some of the daughters aspired to careers in the arts or show business, and the critical mothers balked at the possibility of their female offspring's becoming well known or even achieving celebrity status.

"My mother had my whole life planned the minute I was born," said one woman. "I was the youngest of three, and my two older brothers were going to be the first in our family to go to college. My parents are second-generation Hungarian immigrants, and both sets of grandparents plus my parents were going to pitch in with tuition and make sure the boys got an American education and a shot at the American dream.

"Me? Nobody was going to spend any hard-earned money sending a girl to college. I was supposed to learn domestic skills at my mother's knee, as well as feminine wiles, and then land a good husband. But I had other ideas. I wanted to be a fashion editor or a fashion designer. I had no idea what either of those careers entailed, but I just knew I had a knack for drawing and an eye for fashion, and it all seemed so glamorous. I had seen a movie when I was a little girl about this famous fashion editor, and I had decided that was my dream and I was going to make it come true. I sketched all the time, and I begged for art lessons, but my mother told me I had my head in the clouds. So I saved up my allowance for sketchpads and pencils and charcoal and self-teaching art books. Once, when I stayed out past my curfew, my mother went into my room and rummaged around among my personal things until she found my sketchpads. She burned them. When I got home, she screamed at me and wanted to know what I was doing out with some boy until after midnight. She called me a whore. Then she grounded me for three weeks.

"I tried to talk to my father, but he had no time for me and my crazy dreams. He would just say, 'Listen to your mother. Don't make waves. You've got a good life. People have it worse.' "

This woman eventually married quite young in a hasty attempt to escape from her parents. Her husband proved to be a male version of her mother, autocratic and unloving. But she had children in short order, and by the time she was thirty, she says, she "felt as though I had died before I ever had a chance to live." That was when she met the man who became her long-term lover. He was her art instructor at the local community college where she signed up for a continuing education course, against her husband's wishes, paying for the course with a little money she had won playing the lottery. Over the years—almost twenty at this writing—the lover has given her the support and encouragement and affection she has never gotten from anyone else, and they have been sleeping together for the last fifteen years. But she says she's "not really in love with anybody except my children. I'd do anything for them. I'd die for them. I stay married mostly because of them. I also stay married because I don't really want to marry my lover. He's terrific, but sometimes I wonder what would happen if we got married. Would he change? Would he start bossing me around? That's all anybody I've ever tried to love has done to me. I'd rather not risk it. We're fine just the way we are, kind of at arm's length emotionally, if you know what I mean."

——

This woman, along with Lily and many other women in this chapter, is reacting in adulthood to what amounts to the figurative absence of one or both parents during childhood. That is, the families these women grew up in were not "broken homes," but the parents were emotionally unavailable or overbearing or both. This seems to me an extremely important point, given what David Popenoe, associate dean for social and behavioral sciences at Rutgers University and cochairman of the Council on Families in America, has dubbed the "Great Family Debate of 1992." He is referring, somewhat obliquely, to the Dan Quayle/ Murphy Brown flap which escalated during the 1992 presidential campaign into a full-fledged issue, popularly called family values. The debate was spawned by a fictional TV character who chose to have a baby out of wedlock as "just another life-style choice."

In an impassioned essay for the op-ed page of the *New York Times* during December 1992, Popenoe made a case for what he called "The Controversial Truth: Two-Parent Families Are Better." Actually, while I sympathize with and applaud people who are managing to rear children in nontraditional families, I couldn't agree with Popenoe more. The same goes for all the women I interviewed for this book, wives who have gone to any lengths to save their marriages even as they desperately try to live lives commensurate with their own talents and needs.

There is another truth, however, and it is a very sad one. While the *ideal* of the two-parent family is certainly better than are the other family forms now so common, many two-parent families are travesties. On the least damaging level, there are people like Lily's parents and those of the other women we've heard from thus far in this chapter. These families might not even qualify as "dysfunctional," but their day-to-day bickering and nagging erode the self-esteem and impede the healthy development of the youngsters they purport to nurture. And the problem then moves to the next generation, as women like Lily fail to make complete, healthy attachments as adults and often, also like Lily, fail to feel ready for parenthood. Who knows how many of the best and brightest women (and men) have not contributed their genes to the future of humankind, simply because faulty parenting in ostensibly intact two-parent families has left them unable to summon the courage to become parents themselves?

Still, the plight of Lily and those in similar families pales in comparison to some of the other domestic scenarios I heard about during my interviews for this chapter. Some of the women I spoke with were orphans or foster children. Others had absentee fathers after a divorce—men who refused to send child support checks and who emotionally abandoned their children as well. Other women were physically abused or sexually molested as children by family members. The women subjected to such horrors, not surprisingly, turn out to be on a permanent quest for affirmation. At the same time, since they know all too well the pain, panic, and humiliation of rejection or worse, they have chosen not to put all their emotional eggs in one basket. The two-track pattern, with a marriage plus a long-term lover, is a natural for these women since it gives them a sense of safety, a sort of backup man in case one or the other of the relationships fails.

Yet ironically, precisely because these women never fully give themselves to anyone, many of them end up with no one at all. More of them than the women in previous chapters got divorced eventually, although none of them wanted to, and of those who got divorced, a substantial number have ended up without the lover as well. Typically, the men pull away, feeling the lack of true commitment, but sometimes the women push the lovers away when these men start demanding exclusivity.

Fortunately the positive side of this tangled problem is that these women are laudably self-sufficient, both in the practical sense and in the emotional sense. They are "nobody's baby" in that they are able to take care of themselves and handle their worldly affairs, and they also have great inner resources which allow them to experience being alone as pleasurable, a kind of peaceful solitude rather than an empty loneliness. Even so, the flip side is that they are also "nobody's baby" in that they do often end up by themselves. Many of them are not only divorced and not seeing anyone but also childless. Quite clearly their fear of attachment is one factor which has kept them from choosing to become mothers.

There is a certain undeniable poignancy here, of course. I found it touching to hear these bittersweet life scripts born of what I call "parent hunger." To the outside world, a woman who has suffered from parent deprivation can appear feisty, clever, successful, witty, and able to stand on her own two feet. But not far under the surface is a little girl who has learned a hard truth far too young: You can lose forever, in fact or in spirit, someone you thought was always going to love you and take care of you. The solution these women have found is never again to entrust another person completely with their love. But remember that even here the desire to make the marriage last and to protect the children, if there are any, is paramount. And the pain these women feel should their marriages fail is exquisite in its agony, precisely because they had consciously or unconsciously hoped against hope to give their own children the kind of secure and loving environment which they themselves never enjoyed. To understand how this fits in with the fact that these women have also dared fly in the face of traditional mores by maintaining long-term love affairs, let's listen to their stories just as they told them to me. First, meet Margaret, now sixty-eight and living alone:

"I remember the accident as if it had happened yesterday. I was driving, and my mother was in the front seat next to me. We were on our way to St. Louis for a day of shopping. I was nineteen, and I adored my mother. We got along almost like girlfriends. I know that's unusual, but even when I was teenager, our relationship didn't change. She was so open and funny and young at heart. We talked about sex and everything. And I loved our special trips together. We'd try on clothes, use all the perfume testers, and have lunch at a fancy restaurant. She always ordered a club sandwich. She just thought that was very chic for some reason.

"We lived in a small town about two hours from the city, so our jaunts seemed so glamorous. We'd talk about how I would maybe move to the city when I grew up, but I would say she'd have to come with me because I'd miss her too much. I would tell her that we'd get a little apartment and be roommates. Of course, we left it unsaid that she'd have to unload my father first, which I privately thought would have been a wonderful idea. He was a tyrant, a loud, mean dictator, and I couldn't stand him. Neither could my older brother, and his solution had been to spend most of his high school years camping out on various friends' davenports. He was almost never home. Then he left for college, and he never even came home for the holidays.

"But back to the accident. We were driving along the highway, with cornfields on either side. It was one of those incredibly hot summer days, and we passed one field of popcorn and the corn was popping right off the cob. We got hysterical laughing, and we were having the best time. Then we started reading the Burma Shave signs out loud in unison. I guess you had to be there, but it was really funny at the time. I was thinking about how I loved her so much and how I might dare suggest that she should divorce my father and start over with me in the city. Then, out of nowhere, a car was coming at me. It swerved in and out of the other lane, and then there was the impact. We were smashed backward into a telephone pole. There was glass everywhere. And blood. I passed out after that. When I came to in the hospital, my father and my aunt and uncle and cousins were there. I was OK except for a mild concussion, whiplash, and lacerations. They waited until the next day to tell me. My mother had internal bleeding. She died. She died before I came to. I never even got to say good-bye.

"I never felt any guilt. The other driver was drunk. There was nothing I could have done. But the grief was so deep I can feel it still. She was an angel. I lost my mother and my best friend. I went a little wild after that, dating every guy in town. I had a job at the soda fountain, and all the cute guys would come in and I'd make them Tin Roof sundaes on the house when the boss wasn't looking. I could have had any one of those guys. Up until then I had done everything but go all the way, and then I did it with one guy, and after that it was easy. Then I got kind of serious about one guy, Donny. He seemed to be everything my father wasn't, and I put my trust in him. Pretty soon we stopped seeing other people. He gave me a heart-shaped locket with his picture inside for my birthday.

"That summer I went to Hannibal to visit my second cousin for a couple of weeks, and while I was there, she fixed me up with a nice gentleman five years older than I was. His name was Wayne. Wayne and I double-dated with my cousin and her boyfriend. I found him to be very polite and pleasant. He was a haberdasher, and he had never been in the war because he had hurt his knee in a high school football game. Then at the end of the first week I got a letter from Donny. He was engaged. He had gone back to the girl he had been dating before he met me. His parents liked her and knew her parents.

"I was stunned. I don't know whether I wanted to marry Donny, but I know I had been convinced that I could have if I'd wanted to. So I got very serious with this gentleman, Wayne. At the end of ten days we decided to get married. We had a civil ceremony, with my cousin and her boyfriend as witnesses.

"Wayne was a lovely man. My mother would have liked him. He treated me well, and he was kind of like my mother actually. He had a good sense of humor, a sense of fun. He wasn't much of a lover, though. He wasn't all that interested, and the missionary position was his entire repertoire. This surprised me since I thought he must have had some experience. He was five years older than I was after all.

"So life went on, and we had three children, two boys and a girl. Wayne started working extra hours because our expenses were so great. He was an honorable man, a good provider. I had no complaints. I never really felt much for him, though, to tell the truth.

"Just after our seventh anniversary I gave a birthday party for our five-year-old daughter. A gentleman came to pick up his daughter, and I saw him standing there, very dapper, and I wanted him. I acted very charming, and I asked him in, and we chatted while we got his child ready to leave. I sent out signals, if you know what I mean. He called me after that, and we saw each other for a year before we went to bed together. His name was Richard, and he was married and had three girls. I never really knew what his profession was. Our relationship was outside of reality. We never discussed substantive issues. I liked that. I felt very safe, somehow, having my nice husband and this other nice man, and I never felt really attached to either one of them. That was my little secret. And it wasn't a guilty secret at all.

"This went on for close to fifteen years. Then Richard announced that he was getting a divorce. I panicked. I had never imagined that he might be free to claim me. I didn't want that.

"Not long after that my husband found out about Richard. I had left my diaphragm in the glove compartment. How could I have been so stupid? I had been so very careful to keep things secret, but just that once I left a clue. Well, my husband found the diaphragm, and he left a note on the seat asking who I was seeing. I mean, Richard and I never made love in the car, and it didn't take a genius to figure out what was going on. After that I broke off with Richard immediately. He called and called, and finally he gave up. This was a great sadness for me, a very great sadness.

"But I had given up Richard too late. Wayne was disgusted with me. We divorced two years later. The children were grown by then, so it wasn't so bad. But it wasn't what I had wanted. Nobody needs me.

Maybe I could get Richard back, but I'm too tired. I wanted to have a golden wedding anniversary with Wayne. I never had a real wedding, so I thought we'd have this wonderful party.

"I'm not asking you to feel sorry for me. I brought this on myself. And I don't regret the years with Richard. Also, I'm okay by myself. I have some family money because my father died, so I'm all right on that score. I've got my own apartment and I love it—a cute little place, easy to clean, no one to bother me. I have my women friends over for bridge; I eat out a lot; I watch TV; I do needlework.

"Two years ago Wayne got emphysema—he was a heavy smoker—and when he was in the hospital dying, I was at his bedside. I just had to go and see him. We had our farewell. He was a good man.

"I'm fine now. Maybe I'll have grandchildren. My kids have been in no rush to get married and settle down, which I think is really smart. But they will someday, I imagine. For now I have my own life. I like fiddling with my finances. I've started playing the stock market, and it gives me a real high. So I have no worries. I look at some women my age in these awful marriages, and I know they envy me my freedom. Somebody tried to fix me up with a man from the church last week, and I just said I was busy. I don't have the energy to get involved again. Look at it this way. Even if I had stayed married, I'd be a widow now. So I'm just going to leave well enough alone."

———

There were many, many stories similar to Margaret's. Like her, the women in this chapter grew up with a paucity of parenting and thus had great difficulty in attaching to others later in life. While the women in this group were as fiercely determined as those in previous chapters to make their marriages work, they often simply lacked the skills or the ardor to make that happen. For the same reasons, their affairs never came to fruition either. The solution for many of these women was to fill the resulting void by channeling all their energy into work of some kind, whether a full-fledged career or volunteer work. For Margaret, the "work" was handling her own finances for the first time. She said to me that she "gets high on money more than on men." In this way Margaret and the others we are about to meet are more like traditional males who may have had wives and mistresses but who gave more at the office than they ever did anywhere else. This is not to say, however, that these women felt no regrets. They did make peace with their single status, but they all were saddened and even amazed that their marriages had failed. They also were sorry that their lovers had left them, since like the other women in my study, they typically got a great deal more companionship, friendship, and good sex with their lovers than with their husbands.

But in the end many of these women let both relationships slip away. As one woman said, "I wish I had someone in my life who would say to me, 'No one can take your place.' I've never felt that I was important to anyone—certainly not to my mother or my father. I was a 'menopause baby,' an accident, and my parents never hid that from me. My two older sisters were already in college when I was born, and my parents had been planning to travel and have a great time. Then they got saddled with me. Mostly they ignored me. They had done the whole kiddie thing, and they weren't prepared to do it again. I had only one birthday party, when I was six, and that wasn't even at home. My mother took two of my friends and me to Burger King. She looked bored the whole time, and I remember thinking we should hurry up and finish eating.

"The other problem is that I'm mildly learning disabled. This is so odd, but I've always felt guilty about that. It made me even more of a burden on my parents because they had to pay for tutors and worry about whether I'd ever get into college. My sisters were straight A students, so this was all new to the family.

"Well, I never went to college. I got a job as a pattern cutter in the garment district in New York. I was dying to go to the Fashion Institute of Technology, but I figured I'd never get accepted. So I kind of learned the trade on the job. Then I married the first guy who asked me. He was okay. But I still had that sense that I was dispensable, that I could easily be replaced. I had a lover for fifteen years, but I didn't feel any more secure with him than I did with my husband. Two years ago my husband asked for a divorce, and I didn't argue. Then my affair just kind of fizzled. So I'm alone, but I don't mind. I like the peace and quiet. I've never had kids. I don't think I'd be a good mother. The only place I feel important is at work. I'm a seamstress with my own business now, so nobody can fire me. I could lose a customer, although I'm proud to say that I never have, but I'll never lose my business. And my customers say my work is very good, very special. So that's one area where I feel that no one could take my place. At least that's what I tell myself. But I want to emphasize that I wanted to make my marriage work."

Like this woman's story, the following vignettes illustrate how a deficit of good parenting can render people unable to love and, in these cases, cause them to try to juggle two-track love lives in the hopes of always having someone, only to fumble all their options in the end.

———

❧**Coreen, fifty-three:** "My father died of a heart attack when I was seven. Then my mother died in a car accident when I was nineteen, just six months before my wedding. My fiancé, Scott, was very supportive, and we went ahead with the wedding. I had thought I would collapse into Scott's arms and feel safe after all I had been through, but somehow I never got all that close to him. Then I met Chuck, and he was good to me, and I saw him for eight years off and on. I don't know what I was looking for, really. Chuck was a wonderful friend, and eventually we started sleeping together. But I didn't really love him. I had no intention of leaving Scott for him. Then, one day, I got the shock of my life. Scott and I were making small talk during dinner, and he suddenly said, 'There's something important I have to tell you. I don't love you anymore. There's been nothing between us for years. You know that. And I'm in love with someone else. I want a divorce so I can marry her.' He was totally calm and matter-of-fact. It was absolutely surreal. And I didn't cry or react at all. I just sat there for a long time. And then I just said, 'Okay.' I wanted to fight to keep him, but I couldn't find the words. He had presented this as though it were a fait accompli.

"So my marriage failed. We never had any children, so at least there wasn't that to deal with. Now you might think I would just turn around and marry Chuck. But I didn't. Maybe I was afraid of getting burned again. I don't seem to be very good at relationships. So I broke off with Chuck altogether. I dated for a while, but now there's AIDS, so I've stopped seeing men. The big news is that I'm going to college. At my age! I've been a secretary all my life, and the place where I now work has a plan that pays for employee education. I can fit in only a course or two each semester, but I love it. I really look forward to the evenings I have classes. Then I have all my studying to do, and I'm an avid gardener, and I belong to the women's group at my church. This year I'm in charge of the fall fair, which is a tremendous amount of work. So I keep busy. I'm never lonely. I've had the luxury of being by myself for so long at this point that I don't think I could adjust to living with anybody else."

———

♪Donna, forty-one: "My father was a tough disciplinarian, and he ruled our whole household. I was terrified of him. I always tried to be the best little girl in the world. My sister was the opposite. I could never understand how she had the nerve to rebel against him. He never hit us or anything. It was just verbal. He put us down all the time. But you know, I once read a quote by C. J. Ducasse that said, 'To speak of "mere words" is much like speaking of "mere dynamite." ' That was true for me. The words really hurt me. Then, on his deathbed, my father said he loved me. That was the first and only time. And through all this my mother was just this little mouse, totally subservient.

"Anyway, I don't know why I'm telling you all this. You asked about the men in my life. Well, I can make a long story very short. My first husband turned out to be a coke addict, so I divorced him really quick. Then I married a nice enough guy, but not long after that I met Jeremy.

He was a traveling salesman—no kidding—and he came to the office where I worked. That happened maybe three times a year. He was fifteen years older than I was. We started seeing each other, going to a hotel, every time he was in town. He made me feel so good. He said nice things I had never heard before. And I had this whole fantasy life about Jeremy's taking care of me forever. But I knew it was just a fantasy. Life went on like that for about ten years, and then my husband had an affair which I discovered. I was so hurt by that. I know this sounds funny, since I was seeing Jeremy, but that's how I felt. Like I couldn't trust anyone. Betrayed. I never have been able to trust anyone.

"Not even Jeremy. Once I was single, he backed off. I guess he was afraid I would press for a commitment. Maybe I would have. But it doesn't matter. I'm happier now than I've ever been. I don't have the urge to get seriously involved again. I'm exhausted. For me, close relationships always have a lot of conflicts. It's just not worth it. I've gotten really involved in work, and I am now the boss's private secretary. It's a great job, and I'm very good at it if I do say so myself. I'm also thinking of starting a word-processing service of my own. I got the idea from some ads I saw in the back of a magazine. There are people who prepare manuscripts. I could do that easily. Wouldn't that be a high! I can just picture having my own business cards and stationery printed, making a budget. I'd be totally in control. The more I worked, the more I would earn. Just talking about this gives me the shivers I get so excited. More excited than I could ever get about a man again, that's for sure!"

<hr/>

❥**Marlene, thirty-five:** "When I was eight years old, my nineteen-year-old cousin sexually molested me. It was horrible. I never told anyone. But I always thought that my parents *knew*. They were my parents after all. They should know everything. They should have protected me or at least made me feel better. This was just the way my mind worked at that age. I was terrified of my cousin after that, and I couldn't believe it when my parents suggested he should be my baby-sitter again. I got hysterical crying. They just shrugged and got someone else. They never asked questions. So I stopped trusting my parents. I decided that they really weren't my parents, that I had been adopted, and that my real parents would have been able to keep someone from hurting me. Eventually, of course, I kind of forgot the incident. It came back to haunt me when I had intercourse with my first boyfriend. I just pulled away and said it hurt, and he stopped dating me. Then, at nineteen, I married a nice man who thought I was a virgin. He was very gentle with me, and I got so I could handle it. But I never really loved my husband. And I had it in the back of my mind that he was going to leave me someday. I don't know why. Then, when I had been married for four years, I met a sweet guy at work. We started having an affair, and it's been ten years now. He says he would leave his wife and children for me. I doubt that that's true. But I like to think it is. It gives me a safe feeling. It's nice to think that somebody is always there for you, even if it's a kind of fantasy. But I'm not counting on anything's lasting forever. I'm superstitious or something. That's why I've always worked and always had good credit in my own name. If I ever ended up alone, I could take care of myself."

‒‒‒‒‒

❥**Deanna, fifty-two:** "My husband, Walter, is a wonderful guy. We've been married for thirty years, and I know I should have no complaints. The one thing is that he has a certain subtle way of putting me down. But hey, a lot of men do that. It's nothing compared with what I went through as a child. My father was a raving maniac, and I was always black and blue or burned or something. My mother just closed her eyes to it. But you would have thought somebody, some teacher, would have figured it out. Like my ballet teacher maybe. All you wear is a leotard and tights, so she could see what was going on. I guess people just don't want to get involved.

"I didn't hold it against her, though. That ballet school was my salvation. You know that song [lyric] from *A Chorus Line:* 'Everything was beautiful at the ballet'? That's how I felt. I loved everything about it—the music, the joy of movement, even the sweat and the discipline. I never had much talent, and I never got solo roles or anything, but it was my safe place, a kind of dream world.

"I stopped dancing when I was in high school. My father insisted that I keep my grades up, and he said the dancing was taking up too much of my study time. I was heartbroken, but there was nothing I could do. I ended up salutatorian of my class, and he gave it to me for not being valedictorian. And he said I had to go to a state school and live at home because it was cheaper. The thought of four more years in that living hell was more than I could stand. So that summer I went all the way with Walter. We had dated some in high school. I got pregnant. That was what I was hoping for. And Walter said he'd marry me. What was my father supposed to do? I had outsmarted him. Walter and I lived in married student housing on his campus, and his parents paid the bills. After graduation Walter got a job in circulation for a magazine, and we had another baby. I loved being home with my kids, and since I had read all this stuff about child abuse and how it can go on into the next generation, I was extra careful to be the perfect mother. Still, Walter has this way, as I said, of putting me down. There is always something wrong, just some little thing.

"Then, when we had been married for ten years, I saw an ad for adult education courses at the community college. There was a beginning ballet class two evenings a week, and I just had to go. Walter agreed. He said maybe I'd lose my baby fat. He meant the weight I had gained with my pregnancies. So I signed up, and I was terrified and excited at the same time. I wore sweatpants because I was embarrassed about my body. But I shouldn't have worried. Everyone else was in just about the same shape, and they really were beginners. So I was the star! I was stiff and out of shape, but I remembered all the steps, and it was the greatest feeling! After about the third class I was picking up my dance bag from under the piano where we all pile our things. I stood up, and the piano player, a handsome young man named Josh, smiled at me. I smiled back, and we just stood there for a minute. Then he said, 'You're a lovely dancer. I enjoy watching you. You have such a sense of the music.' I was overcome. What a wonderful compliment. And it was true that even when I was a little girl, even though I wasn't the best in the class in other ways, my teacher had always said I was very musical.

"Let me get to the point. Josh and I started going for coffee after class. Things stayed at that level for about two years. Then we started sleeping together. He always makes me feel so beautiful and so talented. We've been together for twenty years. He's married and has two girls. But when we're together, he never mentions them. We are in our own little world. I guess we'll go on like this forever. But you know what? If I'm really honest, I have to say that my dancing gives me more pleasure than either my husband or my lover. It's a genuine passion. I'm not even a professional, but it's my raison d'être. Once, I had tendinitis in my left Achilles', and I was out for weeks. I got panicky. I couldn't imagine not dancing anymore now that I've found this love again. I started going to the classes just to sit on the side and be in that atmosphere, hearing the music and the teacher's voice. I couldn't stay away, even though watching and not being able to dance was painful. Eventually, thank God, I got better. I'm going to dance until I'm ninety-two, I swear I am!"

———

❦Shana, thirty-two: "I don't know my natural parents. I grew up in three different foster homes. I'm told that my mother was white and my father was black. Actually, I had an okay childhood. I was always treated well. When I was eighteen, I joined the army so I could get an education and see the world. I had lots of men in my life. I like men. I always have, especially older ones. Eventually I got married, and we were stationed in Germany. My husband is nine years older than I am. Then I met a man fourteen years older. I adored him. I stopped seeing anyone but him, and I've had these two men in my life for five years now. What one doesn't give me, the other one does. But don't get the idea that I couldn't do without these guys. I love the army; I love my work; I love traveling. I'm very self-sufficient when it comes right down to it."

———

Clearly, as a result of one childhood trauma or another, the women in this group have great difficulty meeting the deep human need for intimacy. Coreen was orphaned; Donna was emotionally abused; Marlene was sexually molested, Deanna was physically abused, and Shana was shuttled from one foster home to another. The common thread here is that these women never bonded in a positive fashion with their fathers, and unfortunately for them, their mothers, even if they *were* still alive, didn't respond to their daughters' emotional needs. What I found so striking, however, was that many of the other women I talked with for this chapter did not suffer from one stultifying childhood trauma. Rather, they endured entire childhoods fraught with the struggle to please seemingly implacable parents. While this may not seem as difficult a situation as the more dramatic ones we have just witnessed, it proved to be equally, if not more, damaging. Certainly, no one has perfect parents. Even so, I was pained to hear story after story of women who were brutalized in their own homes, but in such a subtle way that the teachers and the neighbors and even the grandparents couldn't really put a finger on the problem. And I was touched that the women who were reared in these ineffective homes and dysfunctional families, still grew up hoping against hope that they could make good marriages and make them last for a lifetime. The fact that they so often failed is achingly sad, especially given the fact that they simultaneously clung to lifesaver lovers in an odd attempt to protect themselves from repeating in their marriages the only intimate scenario they had ever known. That, of course, is one in which they were never really loved at all.

The most frequent of the dysfunctional family scenarios which I encountered during my interviews for this book is the one which Lily, whom we met earlier, demonstrated: a demanding father and a weak, compliant mother. Yet while Lily reacted by becoming something of a rebel who resisted ever forming any profound relationships in adult life, a great many more women who grew up in families like hers reacted by choosing husbands exactly like their fathers, in a kind of bang-your-head-against-the-wall behavior. They seem to be saying to themselves: "okay, I'll show you. I'll get this right if it takes me my whole life." Fairly quickly, however, these women lessen the stress of trying to please a husband by finding a lover who, although he is a man, has a personality like the mother. These women go back and forth for a lifetime between the punitive, fatherlike husbands and the more passive, motherlike lovers, and most of them never feel completely happy with either one. Celeste, now forty-seven, is a case in point:

———

"John, my husband, looks so much like my father that it's uncanny. Very handsome, tall, a lot like Christopher Reeve. Nobody could believe I made such a good catch since I'm not much of a looker. At my wedding people were joking and remarking on the resemblance between my father and my husband. I guess John is a lot like my father in other ways, too. He's a workaholic, a very successful engineer. My father is a physician and very successful also. I always admired him. I was in awe of him actually. And I desperately wanted his approval. My older brother, Skip, is brilliant, and he always did well in school even though he barely cracked a book. My father was very proud of Skip, and he always held him up as an example to me. I was a good student, but I had to work for every A minus or B plus, and I used to cry myself to sleep, wondering why I was so dumb, why I couldn't get a better grade point average no matter how hard I tried.

"The other thing was that Skip is really handsome and I'm kind of plain. Skip looks a lot like my father, except he has my mother's blond hair. I don't really look like either my mother or my father. My mother is a beautiful woman. But I have light brown hair, light hazel eyes, sort of sallow skin. I swear, in the summer when I get a tan, I feel like I'm all the same color, just this bland, beige person.

"I tried to talk to my mother about that when I was a teenager, and she was very sweet. But what was she supposed to say, 'You're gorgeous'? I can see in the mirror after all. She did bolster me about my schoolwork, though. She said it really didn't matter if I didn't get as good grades as my brother. She never really expected me to have a career. She had married right out of college, and she's always been the perfect doctor's wife, always doing everything for the family. She never quite lived up to my father's expectations, though. He had such high standards. He criticized her a lot. But she never said anything except 'Yes, dear.' I could understand that. He has this power to make you want to be whatever he expects of you.

"Well, I don't know how I got talking about all that ancient history. I started out to tell you about the man I met after I had been married for four years. My marriage wasn't terrible, but it wasn't great either. I always had the feeling John wished he had picked someone better. He just had a way of making me feel I didn't deserve him. He criticized everything I did: my housekeeping, my cooking, the clothes I bought. He said I wasn't strict enough with the children. He said I should be more outgoing at parties. The trouble was, I thought he was absolutely right, and I'd try and try to live up to what he wanted. But I was feeling so discouraged.

"One day, I was in the supermarket, and a man said, 'Excuse me, I was wondering if you could help me.' I had been concentrating on comparing prices, and when he spoke to me from behind, I nearly jumped out of my skin. Then we both ended up laughing. I liked his laugh. It was warm and genuine. He had a twinkle in his eyes. It turned out that he had been sent to the store by his wife to get a certain brand of brownie mix because she was supposed to contribute something to the bake sale for her son's Scout troop. That brand wasn't on the shelves, however, and this man—his name is Carl—was at a loss about what to choose instead. We started doing this comedy routine about all the claims on the various boxes, and about all the possibilities: with walnuts, double fudge, sprinkle toppings, microwave, conventional oven. We had ourselves in stitches. I suddenly just felt so *good*. This was all so silly and irrelevant, but I don't think I had laughed like that for years. Also, in the end I did give him some advice, and that felt good, too. Someone wanted my advice! Okay, it really sounds like I'm grasping at straws, getting all flattered because somebody wanted my opinion about a brownie mix, but you have to understand, I had never in my life felt I knew anything that was worth anything to anybody.

"I can say all this so clearly now because Carl has helped me see it. We ran into each other, chance meetings around town, several times after the first encounter, and then, as luck would have it, we ended up working together on the Neighborhood Watch committee. It wasn't long before we got something going, and we've been seeing each other for ten years now and sleeping together for the last five. Carl is wonderful and funny and encouraging, and he has really convinced me that I'm not so dumb and not so homely after all. He loves my body, and he has kind of coaxed me to fix up more. I got my hair lightened a little, started playing with makeup, and brightened up the colors in my wardrobe. Just like that day so long ago in the grocery store, Carl simply makes me feel good.

"But I wouldn't leave my husband. Heavens! In this small town? That would be a scandal. Anyway, what has he ever done wrong? Oh, sure, he's still not all that approving of me, and he hasn't really even complimented me on what I think is my improved appearance over the years. But he's basically a fine man and a wonderful father. He is the disciplinarian in our household, and believe me, our kids study hard, come in at curfew, and generally toe the line. I'm grateful for that, given the way so many kids are acting these days. I'm not sure I could handle the kids the way John does.

"Anyway, it doesn't really bother me so much these days that I can't seem to be everything John wants. I do my best because that's just my nature, but when I get that familiar, exhausted, discouraged feeling, all

I have to do is contact Carl. One long, lovely afternoon basking in his attention, enjoying the lovemaking, talking about funny stuff, and I'm all better again. Fortified. Ready to go home and keep making a go of it. I suppose there are people happier than I am, but I can't complain. I've worked things out to my satisfaction. I feel good about myself, better than I ever have before.

"And you know, it just occurred to me that I don't really think about my relationship with my father much anymore. For a long time, when we would go over to my parents' house for dinner or a holiday, I would get all tense and nervous and feel about six years old again. I knew what was going to happen. My brother would be there with his gorgeous wife and their gorgeous children, and Skip and my father and John would talk man talk, while my mother and my sister-in-law and I did the dishes. Except, of course, my sister-in-law is not only beautiful but a lawyer. And her kids are terrific. She does everything, and she does it well. I remember one time when my son had a temper tantrum because he wanted more dessert, and her children were just sitting there like little angels, watching the whole scene. My husband said, 'For God's sakes, Celeste, can't you make your son behave? Haven't you taught him any manners?' All of a sudden, since the child was misbehaving, he was exclusively 'my son.' That's the kind of subtle way John has of putting me down. And it works.

"Or it used to. Now that I have Carl in my life, I'm pretty much immune. I may not be perfect, but there's somebody I can run to who will make me feel *good*. That's so little to ask, but it's everything to me."

———

Clearly, Celeste has been more successful at establishing and preserving intimate relationships than were the women with more severe childhood traumas. But her need to win approval has become a life sentence, one that keeps her from developing enough self-respect to be able to form truly reciprocal love relationships. Her relationship with her husband is simply a repeat of the one she knew with her father, and her relationship with her lover mimics the one she has with her mother. While Celeste has made this work, it is not a truly healthy pattern. And yet, sadly, I heard many, many similar stories. Also, as mentioned earlier, I heard many stories in which the mother was the critical parent and the father was weak or distant, and interestingly, the women who grew up in these households reacted in just the same way as those who had critical fathers and weak mothers. That is, they sought out husbands who played the role of the punitive parents and lovers who played the role of the weak but more approving parents. Gloria, now fifty, is a case in point:

"My mother used to scare me. She'd tell me that if I got out of bed after she tucked me in, the monster under the bed would get me. Then she'd turn out the light and leave me alone in the dark. I hated her. I had a recurring dream that she was actually a witch. In the dream she looked like a combination of the witch in *The Wizard of Oz* and the wicked stepmother in Disney's *Snow White and the Seven Dwarfs*. One morning after I had the dream, I woke up and I was afraid to eat the toast she had made for my breakfast. I thought she had poisoned it. She shrieked at me that I had to eat, and that just made things worse. My stomach was in a knot, and I started crying, and she said, 'What did I ever do to deserve a little brat like you?'

"I had no brothers or sisters, and my parents were divorced. My father was this really dapper, handsome Irishman, and I saw him only every once in a while, but I adored him. He was just a fantasy really. He brought me presents and sang for me in this beautiful tenor voice. My mother said he was a drunk, but I never believed her. I wanted him to be perfect, so I just decided he was perfect. I thought one day he would come and get me and take me away with him.

"He never did, and when I was fourteen, he moved to another state and pretty much disappeared from my life. I couldn't wait to graduate and get away to college. I worked like a dog in school so I could have good grades and get a scholarship. I had one guidance counselor who really helped me, and I doubled up and got out of school a year early. I did get a scholarship to a good school, and my father sent money for room and board. I majored in elementary education because it seemed like a safe bet, something that would get me a job. Then, right out of school, I married Gabe. He was in law school, and he seemed like a strong person, someone who would keep me safe. Well, he has ended up making a good living, but he is also critical and bossy, and the spooky thing is that sometimes I have that witch dream, only the witch turns out to be my husband at the end of the dream. I wake up shaking and crying. I hate that dream.

"But I haven't had the dream as much since I met Terry. He's on the faculty of the school where I teach, and he's handsome and funny and just has a kind of happy-go-lucky outlook on life. We palled around for three years before we started sleeping together. The sex is great. But the best part is that Terry makes me happy.

"I would never get divorced, though. Gabe has always worked hard, and we have built a life together. We don't have children, but we have a lovely home, friends, and just, well, traditions. Terry is very important to me, but I wouldn't jeopardize my marriage for anything. Actually, my relationship with Terry has strengthened my marriage. It has made it possible for me to endure Gabe's criticisms and bossiness. So I will go on this way forever."

Gloria echoes the themes that dominate the women's stories in this book: Her marriage is a priority, her lover was a friend and companion before the sexual aspect of the relationship started, the sex is better with the lover than with the husband, she is faithful to her husband and her lover and does not sleep with anyone else, her lover gives her a sense of parity and affirmation that she doesn't get in her marriage, and she would choose to have this life-style forever. In these ways she is the same as all the women we've met. What is different is the motivation for the two-track life-style in the first place. Like the other women's situations in this chapter, Gloria's ability to form attachments was thwarted by poor parenting, and she ended up needing two men but never really bonding closely with either of them.

Now we are about to meet a final category of wives with lovers. These are women whose need for secret loves stems from the discovery, often belated, of an essential part of their nature—one they can no longer deny.

6

The Other Woman in Her Life

. . . when I look on you a moment, then can I speak no more, but my tongue falls silent, and at once a delicate flame courses beneath my skin, and with my eyes I see nothing, and my ears hum, and a cold sweat bathes me, and a trembling seizes me all over . . .

—*Sappho of Lesbos*

One afternoon, when I was almost a year into the research for this book, I received a letter from a woman on Long Island. She had heard about my project from a friend of a friend, and she wasn't sure whether her situation was what I was looking for.

"My lover and I have been seeing each other for seven years and sleeping with each other for the last five," she wrote. "This relationship is truly the best part of my life. If the world were different, I might leave my husband, but I'm afraid. A poor excuse, but my lover puts up with it. I guess that's because she loves me so much."

I blinked. *She* loves me so much? By then I had already listened to myriad variations on the theme of married women with long-term lovers, but there was one version I had almost neglected to explore, as Lonnie from Long Island was about to remind me. A forty-eight-year-old self-described "good girl," she had married at twenty-one, given birth to two sons and a daughter, and then, at the age of forty-one, had met the woman who became the true love of her life. Would I be interested in speaking with her for more details?

Two weeks later, on a sultry day in July, I boarded a Long Island Railroad train bound for Oyster Bay, where Lonnie has lived for her entire married life. She met me at the station, looking tanned and fit in her tennis whites, and we headed for her place in a late-model candy apple red BMW. During the trip I enjoyed looking at the lush scenery and the posh Gold Coast homes along the way while Lonnie talked on the car phone. First she spoke to the housekeeper about what to pick up for our lunch, then to her husband at his office about when she might expect him for dinner, and finally to the staff at a restaurant about firming up plans for her daughter's upcoming sweet sixteen party. She let out a sigh as she hung up and turned onto Route 25 A.

"This party is going to cost a fortune," she said. "But you know, Vanessa is our youngest and our only daughter. So Don, my husband, really wants to do it right."

By this time we had pulled into the driveway of an impressive cedar-shingled colonial, handsomely landscaped and with the rhododendron in full bloom.

"We have only an acre of land," Lonnie said as we walked around the back to a redwood deck, where the table was set for lunch. "We talked about trading up, maybe moving to Lloyd Harbor, where you can get two acres right on Long Island Sound, but then it just seemed like too much of a financial stretch. Don is an orthodontist, and he has a very good practice, but we didn't want to tie everything up in property. He'd rather look forward to retiring early and doing some traveling. And, of course, we have two boys already in college, and Vanessa will be next, so you can't go crazy."

The housekeeper appeared with frosty glasses of iced tea, and we sat down in the shade of a huge umbrella. "The other thing is that it's not so easy to move, even if it's not very far away," Lonnie continued. "All of us are really involved in this neighborhood—at the church, the club, the school. And I volunteer at the hospital. Why uproot and start over? Especially when we have such good friends."

She stopped and drew in a long breath. "As you know," she said quietly, "there is one friend in particular whom I couldn't bear to leave." At that point the housekeeper brought out a selection of summer salads from the local gourmet deli. We ate in silence for a while, and then I asked Lonnie to tell me about that "one friend in particular." She looked out across the manicured lawn, studded with an in-ground swimming pool. I followed her gaze. The water, shimmering in the midday sun, had a kind of hypnotic, soothing effect. At last, Lonnie began to tell her story.

"Vanessa was six years old, and she got invited to a birthday party for a little girl in her first-grade class. The family had just moved here from the Midwest, but the little girl's aunt had always lived here. She's single, a very successful lawyer who shares a home with her elderly mother, and since our lives are so different, our paths had never crossed before. But that day, when I brought Vanessa to her niece's party and we were introduced, we just started talking. I was going to leave and pick Vanessa up later, but this woman was so bright and so interesting. We ended up sitting by the edge of the pool, talking and watching the children play."

Lonnie paused, trying to give form to her thoughts. "I wish I could explain what I felt," she said with a touch of frustration. "Obviously I have women friends, and we talk a lot. But this was different, and not just because she wasn't a typical wife/mommy person. It was the way she looked at me, the way she listened so intently and appreciatively to what I had to say, the way she laughed so confidently with a kind of sparkle in her eyes. After a while I felt kind of dizzy, and I thought maybe it was the sun. I felt short of breath, too, yet the sensation wasn't unpleasant."

Lonnie searched my face to see if she was getting through to me. "You know what it's like to be attracted to a man—physically attracted?" she asked. "I mean, whether you're married or not, young or old, you can see a certain guy and you get a little, I don't know, a *thrill.*

Whether you're 'supposed to' or not. Right? Well, this was sort of like that." She paused again, then punctuated her next sentence with little smacks of her hand against the redwood table. "But. It. Was. Different."

That hung in the air between us for a while, and then Lonnie said, "Don't label me. Don't call me a lesbian. I fell in love with a person. In fact, as I told you before, it took me a full two years of friendship with this woman before I could allow myself to let her teach me about sex. It's absolutely wonderful—tender yet powerful." She stopped, lost in a little reverie for a moment, and then went on. "I honestly believe this could happen to any woman. Of course, my lover—her name is Monica—she's never slept with a man. So all right, she has a specific sexual orientation or however you want to put it. But I still sleep with my husband, and I don't feel any conflict. Maybe that's why he has never suspected. He gets his sex, just like always, and since Monica is a woman, we've been able to be very open about our friendship."

I asked her what it was that her relationship with Monica gave her which her marriage did not. "That's easy," she said with a smile. "Self-respect. Don is a good man, a good father, a good provider, and I would never hurt him. But he doesn't regard me as an individual, a person with thoughts and dreams and maybe even talents of my own. Actually, why should he? I was only twenty-one when we got married—he was twenty-five—and I see now that I expected him to take care of me, just the way my daddy always had. In return, I would become the perfect wife and mother. And that's exactly what happened. But Monica has shown me that I have a fine mind, that my opinions are valid, that I could accomplish something in my own right, just as she has. And that I can make love in a languorous, sensuous, give-and-take way that's not totally focused on whether Don has his climax." She couldn't help laughing at that.

But doesn't she ever feel guilty? "Not really," she said. "That surprises even me, given my religious background. But this is so natural, so right, so perfect. How could it be evil to love? And to be loved? The only problem is that my relationship with Monica is making me change so much and to look at things so differently. I'm starting to feel like I want to *be* somebody. But maybe that's okay. Once Vanessa is in college, I could take some courses, see what I'm good at. Don wouldn't mind, I'm sure."

But would she ever leave Don for Monica? "I couldn't do that," Lonnie said. "Look at all this: the house, the garden, everything we've worked for, our place in the community. And the children! And my parents! No. I'd be insane to throw all this away and hurt so many people. Anyway, I love Don. Fortunately Monica understands. So I assume this will go on and on. Although maybe I'll end up a widow, and then who knows? Monica said that once, and she quoted Robert Browning: 'Grow old along with me! The best is yet to be.' Not that I want anything to happen to Don, certainly, but statistically women do live longer than men. I like the idea of looking forward to spending my golden years with Monica. She's everything a dear woman friend can be: emotionally open, talkative, funny, kind. And she's my lover, too. What a combination!"

———

That observation fascinated me. I thought about the rhetoric of sisterhood in the late sixties and early seventies, when women said that as we form relationships, we shouldn't leave out half the human race. Those were heady times. Collectively we debunked the long-standing myths that women can't have genuine friendships . . . that we are always on the verge of a hissing, clawing catfight over a man . . . that we are always competing with other women on some level and always consumed with envy of another woman's looks, husband, accomplishments, children, money, career . . . that we gossip behind one another's backs and are never honestly happy for one another. In consciousness-raising groups all over the country, we bonded and shared our frustrations and underscored a fundamental truth: Women can indeed form profound friendships with one another, relationships that have more mutual compassion and frankness, and sometimes more staying power, than their relationships with men. In fact, some recent scholarly research proves the point.

Stacey Oliker, Ph.D., an associate professor of sociology at the University of Wisconsin, Milwaukee, and the author of *Best Friends and Marriage*, reports that her research shows that friendships matter enormously to women over the long haul. She also says that men have a hard time comprehending the emotional sustenance women find in their friendships.

"Men tend to have buddies they do stuff with rather than having heart-to-heart talks," Oliker says. "They play golf or they bowl or they drink, but they don't talk as much as women do."

Oliker goes on to say that while husbands often complain that women get together and gossip about their men, the truth is that while women do indeed talk about their husbands, the wives are not trying to destroy their relationships but to preserve them. "Women shore each other up, share coping strategies, and help each other figure out how to make marriage work. Women are the caretakers of the marriage relationships, and female friendships are definitely an unofficial support group, a place to get everything from comfort to practical tips."

Actually, the fact that women can be true friends should hardly be surprising. Our mothers, after all, are our original figures of attachment, and if the mother/daughter relationship is at all healthy, the daughter will carry this memory of closeness and nurturing with her into adulthood. Particularly if she ends up in a bad marriage, her spirit yearns for that model of what love should be like. And even if she is in a good heterosexual relationship, she retains the feeling that a woman's love is special—compassionate, unconditional, and not at all about who is supposed to lead and who is supposed to follow. In this regard I am reminded of a passage from Erica Jong's *Fear of Flying:* "Would most women get married if they knew what it meant? I think of young women following their husbands wherever their husbands follow their jobs. I think of them living in places where they can't work, where they can't speak the language. I think of them making babies out of their loneliness and boredom and not knowing why. . . . I think of them farther apart in the first year of marriage than they ever imagined two people could be when they were courting."

One wife I spoke with for this chapter, expressing a like sentiment, said: "I knew from the minute we got married that my life from then on was going to be nothing but doing my husband's bidding. He's not even a bad guy. He's just a *man*, and like most men, he's got to be number one. He's got to have dinner on the table when he wants it, and it has to be food he likes. He won't even try a new recipe if I make one. He's got to have his shirts ironed just so. He's got to have sex when he wants it. He's got to have everything he wants. And we're constantly on the move because of his job transfers.

"The last time we moved, two years ago, was to this godforsaken town in North Dakota. I grew up in Southern California, and this is not my idea of an improvement, believe me. Well, I tried my usual tack of joining a church to see if my girls and I could meet people. During the Christmas fair I ended up cochairing the white elephant booth with a terrific woman who happened to have a life story a lot like mine. She was born in New York City, which she adores to this day, and she wanted to be a Broadway actress. Then she got married, her husband got transferred, and she's been a gypsy like me ever since. We got laughing about how dumb it was that we were running the white elephant sale when neither of us has had the luxury of being pack rats, given our vagabond existence. And we passed the time talking about California and New York, vowing one day to take trips to both places together.

"Then, in January, it looked as though my husband was going to be transferred again. I was at the end of my rope. I just couldn't deal with that again, even though I did think any place would have been better than the town we were in. I called up my friend—her name is Katie—and she came right over that afternoon and we both cried and then I don't even know how it happened but we were in each other's arms and then we started touching each other, slowly, tenderly. This just took my breath away. We didn't quite know what we were doing, but there was an instinct or something. I had the most amazing orgasm, and it went on and on.

"The transfer fell through, thank God. I could never bear to leave

Katie. It's not just the sex. It's the sharing, the true love. She's a woman. She doesn't have to be number one. We are equals. But how could I ever leave my husband? I can't support myself. I have three daughters who love their father. This is a horrible situation. I pray that my husband will never be transferred again. And I pray that he'll never find out.

"Once, when I was unpacking a box I had never gotten to during the last move, I came across a music box that my daughters gave me for my twenty-fifth wedding anniversary. It's a silver bell, and it plays 'The Anniversary Waltz.' I wound it up and let it play until the music got slower and slower and finally stopped. There were tears trickling down my cheeks. The end of a marriage. How horrible! After so much has been invested! You can't get divorced just because life didn't turn out to be the way you thought it would. Anyhow, now that I have Katie, my marriage is much more bearable. If we stay here, I'll be perfectly content to go on with my marriage and my relationship with her. Maybe we'll manage to take those trips to California and New York together! That's my dream."

———

Sounds familiar by now, doesn't it? This woman, like so many we've met in previous chapters, is resisting divorce for both economic and emotional reasons, she is convinced that her affair has helped her handle her marriage, she has a sexually exclusive relationship with her lover but continues to sleep with her husband, she gets great satisfaction from the egalitarian nature of her second relationship, and she wants this two-track scenario to go on forever. Also, like so many of the women in this book, she had developed a deep friendship with her lover before the relationship became sexual. The only difference is that in this case the friendship had the extra dimension that many feel only a woman-to-woman bond can bring.

Of course, I'm hardly arguing that every close female friendship is a potentially sexual one. But I do believe firmly that by opening up the possibility of "sisterhood" and letting ourselves define our relationships with other women rather than accepting the conventional wisdom that says women always compete with one another, we have freed many women who do have a bisexual bent to act on their desires. Actually, a fair number of the women in this chapter insist that they are now certain that *all* women, particularly in mid-life, can be ambisexual. "A penis is necessary for procreation, but not for lovemaking," one woman said. "I'm past being able to make babies, so the gender of my lover makes no difference at all. I wish I knew how many women feel this way but are afraid to admit it."

Other women echoed this sentiment, and we do know that as women approach menopause, the estrogen that has fueled the baby hunger during the childbearing years begins to wane. Plenty of mid-life women, not just those in this chapter, talk about a surge of creativity and ambition, a feeling of wanting to give birth to and nurture ideas now that the life stage of giving birth to and nurturing babies has passed. For many women, particularly those who have maintained their health and fitness, menopause is not so much an end as a beginning. And while some may seek out men—sometimes younger men—to affirm their attractiveness, plenty of others put behind them the notion that a woman needs a man in order to be complete. "Oh, please!" one woman said to me. "I've been scurrying around, catering to men, hiding the real me for my whole life. I don't need that anymore. There's something so phony about the way women relate to men, it seems to me. With my female lover I am absolutely genuine for the first time in my life."

Interestingly, I had no trouble finding women who feel that way to interview for this book. They seemed to have a kind of network, and one woman would refer me to another, so that I soon had a plentiful list of people from coast to coast. As I began contacting them and listening to their stories, I realized that there were many striking similarities between them and the women with male lovers. They shared that strong desire to stay married, and they found in their affairs a wonderful feeling of friendship and respect as well as terrific sex. A great many of the women, like Lonnie, were comfortably bisexual, unabashedly enjoying sex with their husbands even as they delighted in sexual relationships with female lovers. Like the women with male lovers who had no trouble compartmentalizing their sex lives, many of these women were able to be sexual with their husbands and then, at another time and in another place, become a different kind of sexual being. Like most of the wives with male lovers, they had sex with their husbands largely out of a sense of loyalty and duty, while they found sex with their female lovers to be intensely exciting. And like the vast majority of the women in this book, with rare exceptions they had no sexual encounters outside the husband/long-term lover relationships.

"Once I found out how fantastic a female lover can be, it did cross my mind to play the field," one wife confessed. "But then I realized that my lover, Miriam, is so much more than a sexual partner. I don't want to dilute what we have or hurt her in any way. She has given me a lot—a whole new lease on life, to be precise. She deserves to have me as a faithful partner. Sometimes I think about what it would be like to be with her all the time. I think about that a lot actually. It's what I really want. But I can't get out of my marriage. My husband is the superintendent of schools in our small town. We are very prominent citizens. We have three children, and all of us are involved in community activities. Why should I be selfish enough to destroy all of that?"

Virtually all the wives in this chapter, like this woman and Lonnie, said they sometimes fantasized about a future when they might be alone with their female lovers. This is in stark contrast to many women with male lovers, particularly those we met in "I Want Some Body to Love," who had male lovers for primarily sexual reasons and who never fantasized about being with their lovers full-time. The women with male lovers seemed to sense that leaving a husband for another man would simply result in rendering the love relationship into a remake of the marriage. As Gustave Flaubert wrote of his Madame Bovary, "She was as sated with him as he was tired of her. Emma had rediscovered in adultery all the banality of marriage."

The women with female lovers, however, all expressed a kind of freshness and excitement, a certainty that a live-in relationship with the woman of their dreams would never be anything like a marriage to a

man. And in fact, those women with whom I spoke v
divorced to live with their female lovers all told me that
happy—serene, open, with no need for pretense. Th
however, that these women took their divorces lightly.
woman in this book, they had hoped to preserve their marriages. Yet
while they originally had no intention of getting divorced and were
willing to settle for carrying on a bisexual existence for years and years,
some of them simply found that continuing to live a lie with their
husbands was no longer possible. "I was perfectly fine and sexy with my
husband for years," one woman said. "But when you find your true self,
everything changes. Imagine that you discovered some latent talent at
mid-life, some great passion for oil painting or something. If you could
quit your day job, you probably would, even though you had been
perfectly happy before. Ignorance is bliss. But when you stop being
ignorant, when you know better, it's hard to deny yourself."

This woman's ability to be "perfectly fine and sexy" with her
husband for years is actually not surprising in light of established
psychological literature which shows that well over one-third of female
homosexuals are capable of heterosexual performance and pleasure and
that as many as 33 percent marry. Reference to the secret life phenomenon is absent from the literature, however, precisely because these
women, like those I spoke with who are involved with male lovers, are
ingenious about not revealing the existence of their lovers. It is worth
noting here, however, that many of these women do trust one another
with their secrets, whereas women involved with male lovers most often
keep their secret entirely to themselves. This is especially interesting in
light of the fact that homosexuals are still severely punished in this
society. Witness the fact that when Patricia Ireland, the president of the
National Organization for Women, came out of the closet, people were
stunned. Another case in point is Colonel Margarethe Cammermeyer,
former chief nurse of the Washington National Guard, who was discharged in June 1992, after twenty-seven years of service, a Bronze Star
for her tour of duty in Vietnam, and selection as the Veterans Administration Nurse of the Year. Colonel Cammermeyer, who was married for

xteen years and is the mother of four sons, realized late in life that she was a lesbian. And she admitted this without hesitation during a routine background check for admission to a war college. That was the end of her distinguished career. She says she realized her true sexual orientation as part of what she called "a process of self-exploration, understanding how you become a full person."

"I was an old lady before I figured it out, with grown kids," Colonel Cammermeyer, now fifty, told the *New York Times*. And she expresses sadness over being discharged. "I love the wonder and pomp and ceremony, and the system itself, the discipline and morale. I really do love the military. My problem is not with the military; it never has been. It is with the regulation that makes me into a stereotype. . . . What I hope to represent is a part of the normality of being homosexual, of not being in leather or shaving my hair, but rather showing how much we are all alike. If people can see the sameness of you and me, then perhaps they won't have the walls that make it so they have to hate us without a cause."

Colonel Cammermeyer is far from alone in stumbling onto her real sexual orientation during the introspective phase of mid-life. True, in the course of my interviews for this chapter, I did frequently hear some variation on the theme of women having been attracted to females in adolescence and then suppressing these desires in order to conform to the social norm. One woman, for example, told me: "I knew I was different in the seventh grade. I was scared to death. I would buy women's magazines and look at the ads for makeup and shampoo and try to put together a sexy look. I wanted to have a mask so no one would catch on. It worked. I almost fooled myself. I ended up married, but then, when I was forty, I met a certain woman, and I couldn't playact anymore."

Often, though, there was no such early indication of a homosexual orientation, and the women expressed astonishment that an essential part of their nature should flower unexpectedly at mid-life. Anthropologist Helen Fisher notes that from a Darwinian perspective a postmenopausal woman is no longer a pawn to the call of preserving the species, and she is freed by her shifting hormone balance to listen to other urges. Fisher also points out that for most of history—until less than one hundred years ago—not many women lived to be post-menopausal. For this reason, the huge crop of boomers, which is now noisily reaching the climacteric with customary self-absorption and its attendant media coverage, may simply be the first cohort that's bold enough and old enough to experiment with all the possibilities for this stage of a woman's life.

One of those possibilities, undeniably, is divorcing a husband and moving in with a female lover. As we have seen, none of the women in this chapter actively sought that scenario, but well over half of them ended up living that way. This is interesting when we recall that the women involved with male lovers who did get divorced or became widows rarely married the lovers, although they often continued to see them and sleep with them on the same lover's "schedule" they had established years before. As Carla, who is now living with her female lover, said to me, "Think about it for a minute. Two women speak the same language. And if there's no man to fight over, you can get along great. Ginnie and I sit up and talk till all hours; we laugh like school-girls; we make plans to travel and see the world when we retire. It's glorious, and nobody is in the dark about what the other person *means*. Not only that, but Ginnie just naturally pulls her weight around the house. We both cook and clean and so on, but we also both *pick things up*. Did you ever know a man who picked up dirty socks or old newspa-pers and put them in a *place?* I take that back. Gay men are very neat. They're terrific housekeepers. Better than we are. I'm telling you, heterosexual men are the only ones who leave dirty socks on the floor. I'm not prejudiced. It's just a fact."

Carla made her pronouncement at a dinner I gave in my New York apartment for several of those women in my sample who have female lovers. It was a fascinating evening, and the combination of safety and camaraderie inspired the women to open up and tell their tales of "gender-free love." Like Carla, they all expressed a great sense of parity in their female relationships, an ease, a lack of pressure. Listening to them, I thought about myself as an adolescent girl and then as a young woman, needing so desperately to be perfect in order to catch a boy and then a man. My friends and I knew the rules. Never let a guy see you in curlers or without your makeup. Never let a guy see you when you're sick. Always smile; always flirt; always be adorable. Don't be too brainy. Don't wear your glasses even if you can't see a thing without them. Don't, in other words, risk rejection by letting him see the real you. Be a doll; don't be a woman. Don't be a vulnerable human being with foibles and needs and dreams and a persona all your own. All that being so, we really can't put all the blame on the men if our relationships were empty. The men didn't know who we were. For that matter, having spent so much time on the ruse, *we* didn't know who we were. Add to that the inevitable differences in male and female styles of communicating, and you have a surefire recipe for relationship failure. But what these women with female lovers were telling me was that in their newfound relationships they could once and for all drop the pretense. On top of that they could speak the same "language." No wonder, as one woman said, "I found out who I was for the first time in forty-two years. That's pretty heady stuff. I can stand there, naked both physically and emotionally, and she loves me just the way I am. I feel the same way about her. No relationship with a man could come close to this in terms of personal affirmation."

Hearing that, and scores of variations on the same theme from these women who love women, I couldn't help relating their special kind of late blooming to the way heterosexual women often take so very long to know and value themselves. I believe the majority of women share this sad secret. For me and the women I grew up with, it wasn't just the ruse with the curlers and the perfect makeup, a trap set to snare a man. We were never ourselves anywhere. We were pleasers. What did our parents want? Our teachers? Our bosses? Whatever it was, we tried desperately to comply. Yes, a certain amount of etiquette and formality keeps society going, but no one should have to lose herself completely in the game of being who she's expected to be and not who she is.

Actually, when that happens, everybody loses. I, for one, know that as I grew and changed, often painfully over the years, my relationship with my husband became richer and more egalitarian. An intimate human relationship isn't two halves becoming a whole. If you start with two halves, you end up with two halves. But if you start with two whole people, you get a relationship that is bigger than the sum of its parts. Thankfully, though, some of us who married young and incomplete have been able to evolve into whole people and retool our relationships for the better. There is a genuine sense of rebirth when this can happen.

If that is so, imagine how intense the sense of rebirth must have been for the women in this chapter who say they have evolved to the point where they can fall in love with a person regardless of gender, as well as for those who believe their true sexual orientation was suppressed for most of their lives. As one woman said, "I felt bad and nasty from junior high on. I was attracted to women, but I knew that was 'wrong.' I wanted to do the right thing, to be good, to be accepted. I put all my energy into forcing myself into society's mold. I used to join in with the other kids when we would poke fun at these two teachers who lived together. Miss Finkel was the French teacher, tall and lanky like Olive Oyl, and Miss Branden was the gym teacher. We used to laugh and call them dykes. I laughed as loud as anybody. When I look back, that makes me so sad. I mean, the whole thing, the pressure we feel to be cookie cutter people, not just about sexual orientation but about everything. In high school I had one dear friend who was an enormously gifted poet, and I remember everyone from the English teacher to her parents telling her that she'd never earn a living that way and that she'd also never be a good wife and mother if she spent all her time pondering and writing. I don't know whatever happened to her. I suppose she earned a teaching certificate, which is what her mother said would be 'something to fall back on.' I suppose she got married and had kids and is living an exemplary life. But it's not *her* life. Which is not just her loss, but everyone's. But then I hope that maybe in the same way that I found the courage to be my true self eventually, maybe she did that, too. But why does this have to be such a struggle? Why can't this culture encourage and reward what is special about each of us instead of trying to homogenize us?"

A good question, particularly since the attempt to make us all the same doesn't work anyway. Women in particular, as we have seen in myriad startling ways, will put up with stereotyping and subjugation only just so long before they find a secret way out, a private path to fulfillment. And women who love women are no exception. Listen to this voice of a good wife and mother who has found her life's greatest satisfaction in the arms and heart of a female lover:

═════

❧Judy, fifty-eight: "I got married at twenty-one because I wanted children. Oh, I loved my husband, but mostly I just couldn't wait to be a mother. I have just always been good with children, and in fact, in college I earned a teaching certificate in early childhood education. I never got a teaching job, though, because my husband, Kyle, accommodated my desire to have kids and I got pregnant six months after the wedding. Kyle had a good job in computers, and I could afford to stay home. The first baby was a boy, and we had two girls in short order after that. I loved those years. We lived in an apartment complex full of young families, and we young mothers had play groups and baby-sitting co-ops and we took the kids to the playground, the zoo, the beach. Sure, there's a lot of work with small children, but mine were all basically easy kids, and I felt as though I was practically on vacation. I mean, my job every single day, as I saw it, was to find an enriching experience for my children, to find a way for them to explore the world and learn. So of course, I got to explore the world and learn with them. I never wanted that phase to end. Maybe I'm just a perpetual kid at heart, but I love being around tiny children. Everything is a first for them; everything is so fresh.

"Anyway, during that time when my children were small, I made one very special friend. Her name was Vicky, and she had two boys just about my kids' ages. Vicky was not as into little kids as I was, and I think I helped her a lot, showing her how to deal with various problems, how to talk to children so they will listen, how to get them involved in creative projects. She really appreciated that. We were together a great deal, and while the kids were in the sandbox or working with Play-Doh, we'd get into long discussions about world politics, philosophy, stuff like that. She was extremely intelligent, and I found her very stimulating.

"In the meantime, my husband was just kind of there. He was a good guy; we hardly ever fought; we made love pretty regularly. I never had any great passion for him, but I didn't really care. My life was just fine, and I had no complaints.

"Then Vicky told me that her husband had been transferred to another state. I was surprised at how totally devastated I was by that news. Suddenly I couldn't imagine being without Vicky. The day the moving van came, I cried and cried in my own apartment, and then I blew my nose and put ice on my eyes and patched my makeup. I went to say good-bye, hoping I wouldn't make a scene. I rang her doorbell. When she opened the door and I saw the apartment empty except for the phone, I was destroyed all over again. This had been her home, the place we had shared so many wonderful moments. Now it was just bare rooms. I stepped inside. I don't know what I was thinking. Vicky was alone, since her husband had left for his new job two weeks before, and her mother had taken the kids for the day so Vicky could deal with the movers. Vicky closed the door behind us, and we looked each other in the eye. Then I found myself embracing her, and I felt a great wellspring of joy and a physical sensation I had never experienced in my entire life. We kissed, and I was transported. Vicky whispered that nothing like this had ever happened to her before, and I said the same was true for me. We laughed and cried and kissed again, and then she had to go.

"We kept in touch, calling each other all the time and writing. Then, after two years, to my great relief, her husband was transferred back to our state. By this time my husband and I had bought a house, and Vicky and her husband bought a house in the same neighborhood. It didn't take but a few weeks before Vicky and I had picked up where we left off, and the orgasm I had the first time I slept with her was the most explosive I had ever known. I felt wistful. I had missed so much for so long.

"I stayed in my marriage and slept with my husband, and she stayed in her marriage and slept with her husband, and we slept with each other. Of course, sex was only part of it. We had so much between us. Vicky made me feel bright and beautiful and excited about life. My husband just saw me as a competent helpmate.

"We went on like this for eighteen years, until Vicky's youngest child graduated from high school and left for college. My youngest had gone to college the previous year. So our nests were empty. We told our husbands about our relationship. My husband suggested he had known all along. He called me a lesbian, and I was confused and hurt. I don't like labels.

"I wanted to stay with my husband, but I couldn't live a lie any longer. Both Vicky and I got divorced, and we have lived together now for over ten years. My children and my mother had a hard time with this, and I am sorry that I caused pain to people I love. But as my mother was dying, she apologized and said she was glad I had found happiness. That gave me great peace.

"Had I known more about myself from the beginning, I might never have married. But I don't know. The urge to have children was intense. I would have had to be artificially inseminated, I think! I still treasure the memory of my years as a young mother, and I pray that my precious children will one day see that I am not perverted, not bad, just living in the way that I am happiest. I think they will understand in time."

―――――

And so for Judy, the pull of the female lover eventually became stronger than the need to stay married—but not until she and her lover had both safely raised their children. Like Judy, many of the other wives in this chapter led secret lives for years with female lovers and eventually left their husbands. While the women with male lovers whom we met in earlier chapters were able to see their affairs as an extension of their ability to love, many of the women who love women found the affairs so dramatically different from their marriages that they could not go on with the double life forever. Indeed, whether the women I spoke with for this chapter stayed married or got divorced, they all said their lovers had shown them their true destinies. Listen to this woman:

════

❯Lucille, fifty: "My mother adored me and and my two brothers and two sisters. I was the youngest. I wanted to please her. I loved her very much. Then, when I was home for the summer after my freshman year in college, she was making my bed and she saw a letter I had gotten from a girl in my dorm. This girl had come on to me, and I had resisted, but she was still pressuring me. My mother was appalled. She confronted me, and I told her I never did anything. She said I was perverted, and I cried and cried. She died two years later during my junior year, and we had never resolved this issue. So the driving force of my life became the need to prove to myself and everyone else that I was normal.

"Actually, even in high school I had suspected the truth about myself. I used to watch the other girls and see how they carried their books and how they flirted with the guys, and I would copy them. I was afraid someone would guess what I was really like. That would have been a disaster.

"I did a good job of fooling myself and everyone else—until that girl in my dorm figured it out. She was a lesbian and made no bones about it. But I still wanted no part of it. During my senior year I started going out with Chet, whom I eventually married. The marriage was fine, even the sex, but he wasn't very communicative. He cared about me as the mother of his kids, period. But I was satisfied. I had proved to the world that I was normal.

"Then, when I was thirty-eight and had been married for twelve years, I met Mary Lou. That was it. I couldn't deny myself any longer.

We had the most wonderful, caring relationship right from the beginning, and we kept it a secret for five beautiful years. I slept with my husband all that time. My relationship with Mary Lou improved my marriage immensely because now all Chet had to be was the stable, appropriate male model of solid citizen, good daddy, good provider, and Mary Lou filled all my emotional needs. I wasn't so demanding of Chet anymore. It was perfect.

"But then he found out. He saw us together in a restaurant, and since she's a woman, I didn't think he'd catch on. But he did. He started asking questions, and I finally broke down and told him. He said he was having an affair with a woman, and he wanted to get divorced and marry her. I was devastated. I didn't want my kids to come from a broken home. But Chet was adamant.

"Now I'm actually glad this happened. I've been living with Mary Lou for seven years. This is true happiness. How could I have ever denied myself for all those years, just because of society and my mother?

"My kids—a boy and a girl—have both accepted this very well. They come for the holidays, and my daughter, who is married and has two kids, just says her kids have two grandmas. Mary Lou is wonderful with the kids, as long as they don't stay too long. She's never had little kids around before. She had been living with another woman before she met me. She broke up with her because she says I am the love of her life. That gives me a wonderful, wonderful feeling."

======

Clearly, Lucille always knew on some level that she could love another woman. But the next three women we will hear from really didn't have a clue that they could get involved with someone of their own gender until the affair actually happened. Two of them said, "It could happen to anyone."

======

❧**Caroline, fifty-five:** "I was introduced to Kathy by a mutual friend. We hit it off immediately. I was pregnant with my second child. After the baby was born, the relationship with Kathy became sexual. It was so lovely. This went on for ten years, and then I felt strong enough to divorce my husband and be myself. I've been living with my lover for three years now, and I'm happier than I've ever been.

"This has been far from easy, however. My husband got the kids after what they always call in the paper a bitter custody battle. He hired a fancy lawyer and 'proved' I was an unfit mother, because of both my sexual orientation and my lack of earning power. He showed that he could give the kids a better life-style. Losing my children was a tragedy. I'll never be quite the same. Oh, sure, I see them, but we were so close when they were little. I was a housewife, a full-time mommy. Cookie baking, play groups, Cub Scouts, Little League, birthday parties, bed-time stories, the whole bit. I wanted to keep being there for them, being their guide through life. Now I don't know how they feel about me. My ex-husband is not a model of tolerance. I wonder what he tells them.

"Also, I wish I had finished college because the financial strain is terrible. I got alimony just long enough to get some secretarial training. Then I had a hard time finding an entry-level job at my age. I had always been so sheltered when it came to money, so this was a big shock. As a child I had everything I needed, and I never worked during high school or the two years I was in college. After I got married, my husband took care of everything financially. He's a CPA, so I just let him handle things. We weren't rich, but we were comfortable, and I never gave money a second thought. Then, all of a sudden, I was on my own. I didn't even know how to do my taxes. I had no credit in my own name. No checking account. I couldn't even qualify to get a telephone number. They wanted my birth certificate and proof of employment. I had no employment, not even an employment history.

"My lover, who had always been on her own, taught me everything. But even so, I worry about money day and night. I did get a job, but the pay isn't much, and I feel like I'm living from hand to mouth. I'm an only child, and my widowed mother is barely getting by on a fixed income, so I have nowhere to turn for help. Also, my lover and I don't live in one of the cities where unmarried couples can register and receive benefits and legal protection similar to the ones married couples have. For example, my lover has the lease on our apartment, but I can't inherit the lease. I'd never qualify for a lease on my own because they do a credit check and salary check. I still don't have a credit line, and I make peanuts. So I'd be homeless if anything happened to my lover. And she can't carry me on her medical insurance, which is unfortunate since hers is much more comprehensive than the one I have at work. Mine doesn't even cover dental and vision, so I'm paying out of pocket for that. You come from a nice middle-class background, and all of a sudden you can't afford to get a cavity filled or get new glasses.

"Still, as I said earlier, except for the money, I'm very happy. I would think that the lesson here is that all women, no matter what, should be better prepared than I was for being on their own. We are so foolish to remain so childlike when it comes to taking care of ourselves."

———

❥Helene, forty-two: "The summer that I was twenty-eight, I was a drama instructor at a girls' camp in Maine. I had been married for three years, and my husband and I both were in graduate school; he was a history major and I was a drama major. I didn't really want to be away from him for eight weeks, but he was busy with his dissertation, and we needed the money my camp job would bring in. Well, it turned out to be an idyllic setting, in the woods on a lake, and I just loved it. At first I called my husband every other night, but then he gently said to me that he really wanted some uninterrupted time to work and that we should take a 'marriage sabbatical.' I could understand that. I started to relish my freedom, going to the faculty lounge for coffee, going off camp with a bunch of the other teachers and counselors. I got along really well with the head swimming coach. She was a hoot. She just had the best sense of humor, and she would keep us all in stitches. After a while she and I started going into town on the weekends together, having lunch and shopping or seeing a movie. She had a car, so we'd take long drives. We'd buy a bottle of wine and bring it back to camp with us, which we weren't supposed to do, and sit on the bed in her cabin and have our little secret party. I felt like a kid again. It was fantastic. So one weekend we went swimming and came back to her room for our happy hour. I slipped out of my wet bathing suit with my back to her, and she said one word, real softly: "Gorgeous." I felt a shiver run down my spine. Then her hands were on my back, gently tracing little squiggly paths up and down. She kissed my shoulder. I still hadn't moved, hadn't turned to look at her. Then she said, 'I love a beautiful back. Smooth skin, firm muscles.' I drew a breath. I still didn't turn around and look at her. But I said, 'Just go ahead.'

"That afternoon changed my life. I still maintain that I am not a lesbian because I enjoy sleeping with my husband, and he and I have since had three children. But I have continued my affair with this woman for fourteen years. During the winter she lives about two and a half hours away. She is a high school physical education instructor, and she has a committed relationship with a female lover. But we see each other about every two months. In the summer we are still both on the faculty at the camp, and my children go there. My husband visits twice each summer. He's a university professor, as I am, and I don't think he suspects anything. He knows this woman is my best friend, and he likes her very much. She is, in fact, our daughter's godmother. Let me tell you, if you had told me seventeen years ago on my wedding day that I would be living like this, I would have laughed in your face. But this has opened up a whole new side of me. I wouldn't have missed this for the world."

———

❧Cara, forty-five: "I am simply amazed that this has happened to me. And now I honestly think it could happen to any woman. The main point is that I was never unhappy in my marriage. I was never even tempted to have an affair with a man. My husband, George, is steady as a rock, a good guy, a good provider, even a good lover. Oh, I have my little complaints, the usual stuff about how he snores and how he forgets to take out the garbage. But basically we've had a wonderful life together. Lots of memories, lots of good times. I never set out to find another love.

"Then one of my three daughters introduced me to a woman. This one daughter is a lesbian, and my husband and I have accepted that. My daughter's friend is also a lesbian. The friend's name is June, and she and I got along famously. But I still never thought anything sexual would come of it. We knew each other for about two years, with endless sharing the way women do, even though she is a lesbian and doesn't have children. She does have a long-term relationship with another woman. We got so we could talk about anything. With my husband— well, he's the proverbial strong, silent type. He just doesn't say much. A relationship with a woman goes much deeper. I've always felt that with my women friends, and it was the same thing with June.

"Then, just as an experiment actually, I asked June to teach me about sex. I think on some level I wanted to understand my lesbian daughter better. June was agreeable, very excited about sharing this aspect of herself. She was a good teacher. And I responded to her right away. I was, as I said, amazed. I didn't think I had it in me. I've always been told I'm a very sexy-looking woman, you know blonde, big breasts, that look men appreciate. I never in a million years would have thought I had lesbian tendencies. I always thought of lesbians as kind of obviously butch-looking women with short hair and no makeup and a masculine manner. But now I wonder if there isn't a little bit of both in all of us.

June certainly doesn't fit the stereotype, and she has never been with a man. As for me, I still sleep with my husband and love it, but June and I have been sleeping together for three years. I don't want this ever to end. My little experiment turned out to be one of my life's greatest treasures. I stay in my marriage for my family and because of the financial security. And loyalty to George. He's a good man, and I wouldn't want to hurt him. But I love June the most. What we have surpasses anything I had ever imagined. I count myself as being very, very lucky that I have found a life with so much richness. I have a husband and family, on the one hand, and a very precious love, on the other—a love that is my private pleasure. Not even my lesbian daughter knows. But every night I fall asleep thanking my lucky stars for June."

=====

Cara and June and all of the other women we've met in this chapter are clearly bound by love in a relationship that is easily as stable and potentially enduring as a conventional, legal, heterosexual marriage. These relationships are, in effect, de facto marriages. For that matter, every woman in this book who is still involved with a lover has formed an attachment of great power and importance, albeit one outside the ken and conventions of a society that continues to acknowledge heterosexual monogamy as the only lawful union between two human beings and to promote marital fidelity as a means of protecting the family unit.

Still, as we have seen, women in all socioeconomic groups and from all religious and ethnic backgrounds and in all areas of the country, whether or not it fits into the accepted moral scheme, have found a way to fulfill their needs and simultaneously maintain the stability of their families. They have gone underground to find a way to live their own lives in secret at the same time that they are living lives of propriety and convention for public consumption. You and I have been made privy to the untold story of countless American women who manage to be one man's wife and, at the same time, another person's long-term lover. Is there anything we can all learn—men as well as women—from the mavericks who dare make a real commitment to more than one love at a time?

7

From This Day Forward . . .

*D*uring the two years when I was doing my study for this book, I personally interviewed 113 women. At one point I had dinner with a longtime friend, and I told her how fascinated I was by what I had been learning from talking with so many women about their secret lives. I told her that my subjects were by and large ordinary women—nice, car-pooling mothers and cookie-baking grandmothers, women from all areas of the country and, in most cases, women with strong religious convictions. I said that I had not known what to expect when I first began my study but that what I had found, over and over, was that women with long-term affairs are not the type who might call in to a tabloid talk show in order to brag about their sexual exploits or make fun of their spouses. These women are not sensationalists. They are sincere and often guilt-ridden, and they live the way they do because they could find no other viable alternative. I asked my friend if she found that surprising. There was a long silence. Finally she confessed that she herself had a long-term lover, one who had saved her from being "emotionally buried alive" in her marriage, and that her fondest wish was that without revealing her secret, she could somehow convey to her two daughters the folly of marrying too young and for all the wrong reasons. With a genuine sense of urgency in her voice she told me how hard it was to get her message through to her girls.

"Sally is eighteen, and Jessica is sixteen," she said. "Sometimes I feel as though they're nothing but swirling masses of hormones. They are hopelessly boy crazy. Well, I should talk. I was married by the time I was Sally's age, even though plenty of people, including my parents, my favorite aunt, my high school guidance counselor, and my pastor, tried to make me hold off and go to college. But I was 'in love' with Jerry, and that was all that mattered to me. Actually, I tried breaking up with Jerry right after graduation, but I couldn't stand it. I started calling him and sobbing, and finally we got back together and I pressured him until he gave in and we went to a justice of the peace without telling our parents. It was, you know, 'A man chases a girl until she catches him.'

"Jerry was twenty and a sophomore in college. His parents kept paying his tuition, but I got a job as a salesgirl in a clothing store to pay for rent and food. My parents were furious, but they did help out a little financially until Jerry graduated and got a job at an insurance company, by which time I was eight months pregnant with Sally and glad to quit my job.

"Looking back, I almost feel as though that wasn't me. That was a totally different person. What was I thinking? I *wasn't* thinking. That's the whole point. I was reacting on some purely animal level. Watching my girls now, I keep trying to remember the intensity of what I felt as a kid. I can't quite recapture it, but I do know that it was powerful, that it was like an invisible force propelling me.

"So I'm dying to be the voice of experience and shake my girls by the shoulders and yell, 'Stop! You're out of your minds! You've got your whole lives ahead of you. Make something of yourselves. You've got plenty of time to find a husband and have kids. Don't get yourselves trapped while you're still wet behind the ears.'

"Actually, I have said some version of that to them, but of course, I'm their mother, just some stuffy old fogy. They won't listen to me. Anyway, they have let their emotions simply run away with them. I'll give you an example. Last Christmas, Jerry and I decided to take the girls with us to Bermuda, which we thought would be a rare treat. We can't afford that sort of thing very often, and I was really excited. So what happened? The girls both started griping the minute we told them about the trip. Sally has been dating a boy named Ronnie for two solid years, and Jessica has been going with Carl for six months, and they acted as though they would die if they had to be away from their boyfriends for ten whole days. Needless to say, we insisted that they come on the trip with us, but they were hopelessly lovesick the entire time, just living to get back to the hotel and make long-distance calls to Ronnie and Carl. One day I blew up at them and told them life was too short for that nonsense. I told them I was going to lay down an ultimatum that they would have to start seeing some different boys when we all got back home. But they just laughed. And then they threw back at me that I got married young and everything worked out great.

"From what they can see, that's true. Jerry's a swell guy. Dull but swell. He's a plodder at work. He makes a decent enough living. He's good-looking. He keeps himself in shape for somebody pushing forty. He's a good daddy. And as for me, I've been a model mom. What the girls don't know is that I've had a lover for the past ten years, ever since I was twenty-six, and that the real me only comes out in that relationship. They also don't know that I'm imprisoned in my marriage both because of all the commitments I've made and because I'm thirty-six years old and I have absolutely no marketable skills. Oh, I could clean houses. I've had plenty of experience in *that* area. But seriously, like the feminists say, every housewife is just one man away from welfare. That's me, for sure. It occurred to me a while ago that I have not paid into the Social Security system since before the girls were born. I have nothing financial in my own name—no retirement account, nothing. That is terrifying.

"Once, years ago, Jerry and I had a major blowup. I don't even remember what it was about. I just remember feeling the emptiness of my life. Being a wife, a mother, was what I was for others. But outside those roles, I was nothing. Right or wrong, I just didn't feel loved for myself or capable of achieving anything in my own right. Anyhow, I grabbed a pillow and a blanket and tried to go to sleep on the living room couch. But I tossed and turned for hours, fantasizing about how I would escape, how I'd take the girls and run away. Yet the horrifying thing was that in my wildest imagination I couldn't devise any *real* plan for how I could pull that off. I am a nonperson in this society. I kept thinking about that Emily Dickinson poem that starts: 'I'm Nobody! Who are you? / Are you—Nobody—Too?'

"I finally got up, put on my robe, made myself some tea, and went out on the deck. It was a beautiful April night, with a full moon so bright that I could see the leaf buds on the maple tree, and the crocuses and tulips pushing up through the earth. All those signs of rebirth, renewal. And yet I personally felt dead. I felt too dead even to cry. I sat there for the longest time, and then another poem came into my head. I couldn't remember who wrote it, but it has one stanza that goes like this: 'I am the master of my fate; I am the captain of my soul.' I started saying those lines over and over, softly. After a while the dawn began to break. And finally I could cry. I didn't know how or when, but I knew that I would find a way to become the master of my fate and the captain of my soul.

"Does it strike you as ridiculous that I eventually achieved that goal by having an affair? I mean, the word *affair* has such negative connotations. But for me, this relationship has affirmed my life, and the beauty of it is that I have not had to disturb my marriage or jeopardize my daughters in any way. My lover is a secret, and he gives me the courage to go on with what everyone else thinks is a happy marriage. Actually, it *is* happy in the sense that my life has a structure and a sense of doing the right thing. And we do make love. It's not exciting, but it's okay. The saving grace is that I have my lover. He gives my life texture. And he encourages me to get a marketable skill instead of being terrified about my future.

"Of course, it would be better if I didn't have to live like this. That's the point I'm trying to make. I want to make sure my girls don't end up like this, just because they think they're 'in love' right now. I want them to get out into the world, get an education, get some traction in the work world, maybe travel a little. I want them to get married with their eyes open. I want them to have premarital counseling, like they now offer at our church, where both the bride and groom fill in these elaborate questionnaires about nuts-and-bolts issues and really face their intentions squarely.

"Maybe I should just level with my girls. But I could never do that. They adore their father, and rightly so. If I told them what I really feel and what I'm doing, I'd destroy everything. I've agonized over this, but I can't tell the truth."

―――――

Remember the woman we met in chapter 2 who wondered why it is that women have not always passed on from one generation to the next the truths we've learned about love and sex and marriage? The woman we have just heard from has given us at least one answer to that question. Yes, in the last three decades we have become much less guarded about breaking the conspiracy of silence surrounding such domestic tragedies as incest, child molestation, battering, philandering, emotional abuse, alcoholism, chemical dependency, and a host of other once-taboo topics. But the effects of so many years of hushing up the horrors linger insidiously. And for many women, telling the truth is tantamount to self-destruction, as well as the destruction of those they love. That is why so many mothers still never talk frankly with their daughters. Woman after woman still goes to great lengths to build up and protect her husband's image, making sure that everyone from the community at large to the children sees a man of strength, conviction, ambition, and character when in fact, he is flawed in one or more ways, often seriously so. I think of TV anchor Joan Lunden, after her much-publicized split with her husband of thirteen years, Michael Krauss, which resulted in her paying alimony to him. Lunden, accused in the press of not doing well enough by the man who had allegedly sacrificed much of his own success to promote hers, told *TV Guide:* "Michael was not my manager. He was not my Svengali. I did projects with him because I wanted him to be a success. I thought that if he were happy, we'd be happy. Instead, I'm in the surreal position of having to fight to keep the right to my own face and my own talent against someone who claims to own a piece of me. . . . I spent so much time building him up during interviews that I'd actually annoy people."

Lunden is far from alone. Human nature being what it is, even knowing that we now have permission to admit what's really going on doesn't always get us past the overwhelmingly primitive defense mechanism of denial or of simply protecting our men in order to protect ourselves. Alicia, still stunning at fifty-three, demonstrates this all too well:

"I didn't get married until I was twenty-four. Thirty years ago you were an old maid at twenty-four. My parents had been in a panic, particularly since my two younger sisters had already married. I was still living at home, teaching third grade at the same elementary school I had gone to. And I was still a good little Catholic virgin.

"Looking back, I can honestly say that I wasn't unhappy. I loved teaching. Mine was not a case of majoring in elementary education for the lack of anything better to do. I love children, and I had developed some very creative ways to get my students excited about learning. I also got the parents very involved. Every fall I would send out a letter that began with a quote from author and child advocate Neil Postman: 'Children are living messages we send to a time we will never see.' Then I would invite the parents to come into the classroom and talk to the children about their careers and hobbies. I would do follow-up lesson plans after each adult had given a 'seminar.' For instance, if someone's mother or father was a newspaper editor, we would have a unit on newspapers and read the daily paper, write our own newsletter, and so on.

"Anyway, I didn't mind living at home. I paid for my room and board, and I had a social life, dating a few men and seeing my women friends for weekend lunches or whatever. But my parents made it very clear that they didn't want me around forever. They wanted me married and out of the house. I finally couldn't take it anymore, and I agreed to marry one of the men I had been seeing off and on for several years. Mike was twenty-eight at the time, and he seemed pleasant enough, he had a good job in the personnel department of a large corporation, and I was fond of his parents. Like my parents, they were relieved when Mike and I announced our engagement.

"It was on our honeymoon that I found out what Mike is really like. He's manic-depressive, and he had been taking medication for this condition for some time. The medication had affected his ability to get an erection. At the time that we were married, he wasn't totally impotent, and we did have a sporadic sex life for almost three years. But after that he got so he couldn't make love at all, so I went without sex for fifteen years.

"Not only that, but the medication isn't foolproof. Mike still has the most amazing mood swings. He manages to hold it together at work, but in private he's completely unpredictable. Sometimes he stays up all night, playing his guitar and talking about grandiose plans to become a famous musician. Other times he's just inert. He sits staring out the window, and he won't let me even try to get through to him. He still sees his psychiatrist all the time, so I guess this is as good as it's going to get.

"Anyway, after we had been married for five years, with my thirtieth birthday around the corner, Mike came right out and said he wished I'd have an affair and get pregnant, since he knew I would be a wonderful mother, and he would never be able to give me a child. I was flabbergasted. But I couldn't bring myself to do anything. By that time my parents and his parents thought one of us was sterile, since we're

Catholic and should have conceived much earlier. I had kind of been hinting about that, in fact, just to cover up the real problem. Of course, his parents knew about his emotional condition, but they didn't seem to know about the effects of the medication. Whatever. I had created this perfect little lie, and I couldn't see any way out of it at that point.

"So I went on like that, happy at work and miserable at home for eighteen years. I was forty-two by then. One weekend a friend of my husband's stayed with us. This man had gone to college with my husband and had since become an executive with a large corporation. Most of the time he lived in Europe, and he traveled a lot. He was very sophisticated, and I was fascinated by him. I don't know what came over me, but after I had had a couple of glasses of wine on the second evening he was staying with us, I approached him and told him that I needed to speak with him privately. This was in mid-July, and my husband was busy with the barbecue. The man—his name is John—seemed surprised at my request, but he went with me on a walk around the grounds of our house. We have an acre, most of it still wooded, and there's a little stream running through the woods, so it's quite beautiful. The sun was beginning to set, and the fireflies were out. My heart began to thud so hard that I thought John might hear it. Finally, I told him the truth about my sex life—or lack of it—with Mike. I wasn't trying to put Mike down. I just had this overwhelming urge to have at least one orgasm before I died. John was very sweet. He told me that he was married but that he would be delighted to teach me to be a sexual being.

"We met at a hotel six months later, when John was back in the States. I told my husband I was going to the theater with a friend of mine, a woman. All the way to the hotel I was a mass of excitement and fear. But once I got there, John took away my fear entirely. We had a lovely candlelit dinner in the hotel restaurant, and then, when we went to our room, he was so gentle with me. The lovemaking was incredible. To think of what I had been missing all those years!

"John and I have been seeing each other about four times a year for the past eleven years. I have never used birth control, but I never did get pregnant. The timing was never right, and now I've gone through menopause. It's okay. I've put all my mothering energy into my school-children.

"And Mike and I just go on. Everyone thinks we're the perfect couple. He still has his mood swings. We never talk. We have no relationship to speak of. But I can't end this marriage. I have no experience in finishing a relationship, so I don't know how to do it. I can't even think of what the first step would be. And I certainly never talk with my lover about what it would be like if we could be together. That would be like wishing my husband were dead, which is horrible. I couldn't even let that cross my mind. Yet I do feel bad that I can't commit fully to him. I said that once, and he said he didn't mind. He said: 'One glimpse of you is worth legions of other women in my life.'

"So I go on with these two men. And I'll never tell the truth. I wouldn't tell the truth to my own children if I had any—even though they'd probably learn something from the truth."

———

As Alicia's story makes painfully clear, facing our own failures and faults, plus those of our spouses, is a very difficult thing to do. Even more difficult is considering admitting our personal frailties to our youngsters in order to attempt to inoculate them against repeating the same patterns as they reach adulthood.

And in fact, maybe some things really are better off not said—at least not directly to our own children. And so how is the truth ever to be told? In a very real sense, the women in this book who have summoned the courage to share their tales of love gone awry for a whole spectrum of reasons have made a generous contribution toward getting the real story out in the open. What we have learned boils down to one extremely important point. That is, the vast majority of the women in my sample—most of whom married very young—talked about "love at first sight." As we have seen, however, there is no universal definition of what being "in love" means, and most often it means being in love with the chance to escape from something: a bad home situation, for example, or simply the responsibility for taking control of one's own life.

However, as psychologist John Money, Ph.D., of the Johns Hopkins Institute has pointed out, three other factors impact on the process of falling in love. The first, without a doubt, is purely feral sexual attraction. But the second factor that influences the process of falling in love is just as important: timing. If a woman is at a point in her life where she is ready to fall in love, she will—whether with a potential husband or a long-term lover. At some other time, when she is busy or preoccupied or striving for some other goal, she will walk right by a suitable prospective mate and not even notice.

The problem here is that very often women are ready for love, but for the *wrong reasons*. Again, the most prevalent reason the women in my sample gave for "falling in love" was to get away from an intolerable home situation. Obviously, if a person is running away to get married instead of moving toward marriage, she is in big trouble. But along with escaping from a dysfunctional family of origin, an impressive list of other bad reasons for marrying surfaced during my interviews for this book:

1. to fulfill one's mother's dreams

2. to get back at one's mother

3. to fulfill one's father's dreams

4. to get back at one's father

5. to have financial security

6. to have a baby either because the woman is already pregnant or because she wants someone to love her

Yet of the women in my sample who were clearheaded enough to resist initial attraction and analyze their own motives as well as those of their fiancés, many still fell prey to the third element in the formula for falling in love at first sight—that is, a barrier of some kind. Thwarted love is, unfortunately, terribly romantic. If a man lives far away, if either or both sets of parents have forbidden the match, or if the man is already married, the inherent drama of the situation often makes people feel great passion. This is what I call the Romeo and Juliet syndrome. Remember, Juliet was a mere fourteen years old when the fatal attraction occurred. And remember, too, that a double suicide is not the only possible tragic end to such a love story. That a hasty marriage for any reason often becomes a life sentence is a tragedy as well, particularly when the resulting union suppresses a woman's individuality and squanders her human potential. A perfect example is the story of a woman I'll call Vera. She married young simply because that was what was expected of her. Like the other women in this book, Vera had a long-term lover but wanted to preserve her marriage at all costs, she knew her lover for some time before the relationship became sexual, she was faithful to her husband and her lover, eschewing any other sexual liaisons, and she found great joy in her lover's friendship and mutual respect. But what is so wonderful is that Vera's story has a surprise ending, one that will buoy your spirits and affirm the words of the writer George Eliot, who wrote: "It's never too late to be what you might have been." Here is what Vera, now seventy-four, told me:

===

"I had a happy childhood in a nice secure family. We weren't rich, but we had what we needed. My parents were both teachers, and they saved up so my brother and I could both go to college. I also won a scholarship, so I went to a good school, one of the 'Seven Sisters.' I met a man from an Ivy League school at a mixer. Everyone said we made a lovely couple. He was to be taken into his family's business, so our future was secure.

"He proposed, and I said yes. I couldn't think of any reason not to do so. Oh, I had entertained some thoughts of a career at one point. As a young girl I imagined being an archaeologist, going on digs to exotic places and making amazing finds that would rewrite history. I also thought of being a newspaper reporter. I would work for the *International Herald Tribune* and be stationed in Paris and travel all over, getting worldwide scoops and winning lots of journalism awards. But in those days career women always seemed to be spinsters. I remember reading a short story in a woman's magazine. It was about a married woman with three little children. She got a call from her former college roommate who was in town on business, and she invited the roommate to her house for tea. At first the story made you feel that the roommate was the lucky one. She was very glamorous in a tailored suit and silk blouse and stockings and pumps. She also wore a hat with a feather and carried a leather briefcase. I forget now what her job was supposed to be, but she talked about her work and her travels, and it all sounded very impressive. At the same time the story's heroine, the young mother, was dashing about, satisfying the needs of her brood, wiping little mouths and bottoms, consoling a child with a scraped knee, stopping a sibling fight, and so on. She was also trying to start dinner in anticipation of her husband's arrival, and she caught a glimpse of herself in the mirror, her hair disheveled and her makeup faded, and she found herself desperately envying her well-groomed former roommate.

"But as the story went on, of course, the tables turned, and we were made to see that the roommate was a lonely, unloved person who hated living out of a suitcase. We were also shown that the young mother was the lucky one since she had her fine husband to take care of her and her darling children to give her life a purpose. The point is that we were made to see this as an either/or situation. You could have a career *or* you could have marriage and motherhood, but you couldn't have it both ways. And since you had to choose, the only 'right' choice, the only 'natural' choice, was to get married and have babies.

"So that's the choice I made. Mitchell and I were married in June right after we both graduated. We went to Niagara Falls for our honeymoon and returned home to the house our parents had helped us buy. I gave birth to five children—three girls and two boys—in a span of eight years.

"I don't know when it was that the sadness began to engulf me. It was a gradual process, and I could never put my finger on what it was that was bothering me. Looking back, I think it was just a series of things my husband did—little things really. For instance, he would read the paper every morning at the breakfast table, and he would read certain news items aloud to me, as though I were so simpleminded that I couldn't ascertain what was of significance and what was not. He also had very strong political opinions, and he would voice them, and this was as good as saying that I had no option but to share those views. I was not allowed to have a mind of my own. I could not disagree with him.

"He also put himself in charge of my appearance. He insisted that I use a different shade of nail polish from the one I had been accustomed to wearing because he thought another color showed off my engagement ring to better advantage. He also advised me on the color I should rinse my hair. I suppose this might sound like flattery, but it was terribly autocratic. I had no say in these matters. I began to feel rather like a doll whom he was adorning to his liking. But what could I do? How would I have supported myself without him? And what grounds did I have for a divorce? That the man chose the shade of my nail polish? Hardly.

"So the years went by. The children grew, and soon they were all in school. I played bridge, and I did volunteer work. And the sadness deepened. You know, in life one must have something to look forward to. That is the key. And I had nothing to look forward to, nothing that made me eager and excited. I knew that eventually there would be my children's graduation exercises and presumably weddings and then the birth of grandchildren. But I would still be playing bridge and listening to my husband read from the newspaper. And going to bed with him, which held no excitement for me at all. He was not a passionate man.

"In 1965 I celebrated my silver wedding anniversary. And I read Betty Friedan's *The Feminine Mystique*. It was my story she was telling.

I cried for the first time in years, great gasping sobs, tears pouring down my face, giving form at last to so many years of sadness. And I made up my mind to do something. I enrolled in a newspaper journalism course at a local college. I was forty-six years old, and I felt like a fool. But I will admit that I have never looked my age, and when the young man seated next to me asked me out for coffee after the second class, I decided not to let him know that I was old enough to be his mother. He was barely twenty! I suppose he thought I was thirtyish, and he saw my wedding band, but none of that seemed to bother him. We had a wonderful time talking, and the next week he asked me again to go for coffee. We were terribly excited about our assignment for the coming week, and we talked about that a lot, and he said I was very intelligent and inspiring. Imagine that! I felt as though he had lit a little flame in my soul, a little flame that had gone out entirely years and years before. Suddenly I was a young girl again, with dreams and a future and—something to look forward to!

"The journalism course was to end after Christmas. My young man—his name is Eric—said he couldn't bear to be without me. We took a long drive one evening, talking about what to do with the rest of our lives. We parked on a lovers' lane the way high school students do, and that was the first time we made love. He was ever so gentle and tender. He took a long time caressing me and arousing me, and he whispered lovely things, and I felt another little flame ignite, one that I had in fact never felt before. The heat grew more and more intense, and when he finally entered me, I was overcome with the most profound pleasure. I knew then that I had never had an orgasm in my entire life until that moment.

"That night I couldn't sleep. I couldn't imagine life without Eric. He had given me, for the first time, a sense of, well, worthiness. I could say the word *I* with conviction, as though I really mattered. I knew who I was. I wasn't my husband's creation at all. That had been a charade. I was a person with a sense of mission and a person with talent. I had done extremely well in the journalism course, and my professor had encouraged me to continue. I was also a sexual being. I had never known any of that. So my life was just beginning, and I was nearly fifty, already experiencing signs of menopause.

"But I couldn't possibly get divorced. After twenty-five years? And as I said, I had no grounds. Talk about the horns of a dilemma! No solution presented itself. And so what happened was that I never made a choice. I stayed married, and I continued to see Eric. He eventually married and became the father of two lovely children. His family became friends of my family. They attended my children's weddings and so on. In the meantime, I bought a typewriter and stole some time to write. Eventually, I sold some articles. This was the thrill of a lifetime. But my husband didn't care one way or another as long as I continued to suit his needs.

"And through all of this Eric and I were lovers and dear friends. Life went on like that for twenty-six years, at which point I was seventy-two. Then my husband died. A year later, tragically, Eric's darling wife was killed in an automobile accident. So there we were, at seventy-three and forty-seven respectively, and suddenly both of us were single. He took me out to dinner on the twenty-seventh anniversary of the day we met, and he popped the question. He gave me a diamond cut in the shape of a heart. We were married that spring, with all of our children and my grandchildren in attendance. We didn't go on a honeymoon because I had a deadline for an article. I loved that!

"So our first anniversary is next week, and I have never been so happy. This man has given me the greatest gift of all, which is the courage and the strength to be who I was born to be, in every way. Now I want to live to be a hundred and five! Or one hundred and twenty! Because at last my life really is worth living."

—————

Vera, more clearly than anyone, demonstrates the danger women face when they allow themselves to lose control of their lives and to become smothered in marriages of convenience. I have a friend who collects bell jars. Then, when she's invited to a wedding, she asks for the little bride and groom statuettes from the top of the cake. She puts the statuettes in a bell jar and gives the jar to the newlywed couple as a memento. This custom of hers is well-meaning, but it gives me the shivers. I see it as a metaphor for marriage itself: a husband and wife in an invisible glass dome, constricted and trapped in prescribed roles for a lifetime. Yes, we've come a long way in the last thirty years, with a great deal of talk about "role-free" marriages, but as we have seen in these pages, the rhetoric has not yet become reality for most people. There is still a need to get rid of the constricting definitions of "wife" and "husband."

We must also scrap the old notion of marriage being the melding of two people into one. How much better for couples to think of themselves as genuine partners, each with an equal amount of weight to pull.

I think of a character in Sam Kean's book *Fire in the Belly.* This man is sitting at a bar, crying into his beer over the breakup of his marriage. He tells a pal at the bar that he doesn't know who is going to go on his life's journey with him. And the pal tells him he has his questions in the wrong order: First he should ask himself where he is going, and then he should ask whom he is going to take with him.

———

That advice isn't bad, but it's strictly from a man's perspective. Women should have a different agenda. There is a very basic question that must come before all others. It is one men take for granted, a notion passed on almost by osmosis from father to son. But even today it is not necessarily one that is passed on from mother to daughter. Women are still left to discover the need for it by themselves. But the trouble is that they do so with shock, years and years after they have made a lifetime's worth of commitments that may well serve to keep them from ever being able to act on the answer to that question, even if they come up with one.

The question is: Who am I?

When a woman can answer that question, she is free to live as a full human being *without* a man. Only then is she truly ready to live as a full human being *with* a man.

How sad that so many women still think the first question to ask is: Who will take me through life with him? That becomes the burning obsession of their lives: finding and keeping a man. Disappointment and despair are inevitable. Instead a woman should ask—*and answer*—the following questions, in the following order:

1. Who am I?

2. Where am I going?

3. Whom do I want to go with me?

If she can answer all those questions squarely, *in that sequence,* she'll stand a much better chance of choosing the right partner and of surviving and thriving in her work, in her marriage, and as a mother. I am hopeful that younger women, if they are reared in a climate of openness and encouraged to find self-respect, may be able to do that. In fact, one woman with whom I spoke recently gave me a sign that there may be a change in the wind at last. Kelly is twenty-one and engaged to the "perfect man." Her parents strongly approve of this match since Donald comes from a good, churchgoing family. He is headed for law school right after graduation. "Maybe he'll become the president," Kelly's mother says, only half kidding. But Kelly says she doesn't want to go through with the wedding.

"I love Donald," she said. "I think I do anyway. He's so sweet, and my mother is absolutely right that he is 'perfect.' I'm the envy of all my girlfriends. But the idea of graduating and getting married right away without ever trying my wings simply terrifies me. I don't have any grand dreams, but I would love to go to New York, get a job as a receptionist or something, get a little apartment with a roommate, and just see what happens. I was in New York over Christmas break with a couple of my friends, and I loved it. We saw plays and ate out and did tourist stuff. We got the Sunday paper, and I saw all these ads in the help wanted section under the heading 'College Grad.' There were entry-level jobs in publishing and advertising and so on. I know I could do it. And who knows what might happen? Maybe I'd get promoted and be a big success.

"I'd also like to travel. I've never even been to Europe. I was thinking of taking off one summer and getting a Eurail pass and going around with a pack on my back and staying in youth hostels. I got a book out of the library that tells you how to go to the UN and get a student discount travel package. The airfare isn't that bad at all.

"I just want to know what's out there. And that goes for guys, too. I've been dating Donald since my freshman year in college. Exclusively. Before that it was just a bunch of geeks from high school. High school boys don't count as men in my book. What if there's some man of my destiny out there somewhere, and I'll never meet him because I get married to good old perfect Donald? I'm serious. Maybe the great love of my life is somewhere besides my little college campus. Maybe he's in Paris. Maybe he's in Milan. Maybe he's just in Chicago or something. But I'll never know.

"What should I do? We've already rented the hall for the reception. We've made the guest list. But I don't want to go through with this! If Donald really is the love of my life, he'll be there waiting for me after I've done a little living. Won't he? What would *you* do?"

―――

I won't tell you how I answered Kelly's question. I want you to answer it for yourself. But I also want you to think for a minute about Donald and about his options and his future. In fact, I want you to think about all the men in this book. First, consider the fact that the husbands who *didn't* meet their wives' needs were themselves living out lives in loveless unions. And then ponder the point that the lovers who *did* meet the needs of those same women, in an overwhelming number of cases, were themselves married. They were thus leading secret lives of their own. Whether their motivations for doing so parallel those of the women we've met in this book, or whether the male experience in this regard is substantively different, will have to remain matters of conjecture for now.

In the meantime, here's to a future in which there will be more husbands and wives who can communicate their needs to one another and therefore far fewer wives who need long-term lovers—but also one in which wives who *do* need lovers will need to understand that there is a price to pay for this form of psychological salvation. But the chances are that two-track relationships will continue to occur. After all, even marriages made with great forethought can end up holding nasty surprises. And even those in which care is taken to keep the lines of communication open can turn out to be unsatisfying. Yet should either turn out to be the case, if there are children and careers and traditions and community connections to consider, as this study shows, women will prefer to avoid divorce if possible.

But I can also guarantee, after listening to so many wives' stories, that women will not allow themselves to face decades of a life not fully worth living. Witness a recent report in the *Ladies' Home Journal,* entitled "The Lovelife of the American Wife." The report was based on a survey of the magazine's readership and served as a follow-up to a similar study done ten years ago. In the decade that had elapsed, the number of wives who reported having affairs had risen a full 5 percent to more than one-quarter of the sample, and the report said that two reasons for the increase were statistically significant. The first was that as women move into the workplace, they have more opportunity to meet men, and the second was that "women are becoming more like their male counterparts: They want and expect sexual satisfaction, and they'll turn elsewhere if they can't get it at home." Of the magazine's respondents—who totaled more than forty thousand—60 percent said their relationships with their lovers are more exciting than marital sex, and 47 percent said their relationships with their lovers have had a positive physical or emotional effect on their marriages. Certainly, these findings dovetail with what we have heard from the women in this book.

They also underscore the truth of the slogan of the *Ladies' Home Journal:* "Never Underestimate the Power of a Woman." This pithy phrase—first coined in 1941—originally meant that the "woman behind the man" was the real, if hidden, power in a relationship. Yet the slogan, over the years, has taken on new meaning. As the women in this book have shown us, women are getting very good at empowering *themselves,* at recognizing their *own* needs, and getting those needs met in whatever way they feel they must. And so, in the final analysis, what does all this mean?

Love is not a luxury item. True love—not the illusory sensation of love at first sight, but the kind of love that feeds our souls and thrills our bodies and lasts a lifetime—is as essential to human life as are water and food and clothing and shelter. When women find themselves trapped in marriages that don't give them that essential kind of love, the solution to the dilemma for many will no doubt continue to be the formation of a secret life with a lover who offers whatever respect, companionship, and sexual fulfillment may be missing from the relationship that was supposed to fulfill the almost impossible goal of satisfying every need for every season and every reason for as long as they both shall live.

I will leave you with the words of Francesca Johnson, the heroine of Robert James Waller's passionate, lyrical novel *The Bridges of Madison County,* about an itinerant photographer for *National Geographic* who stops to ask directions of a farm wife in Iowa. Their almost mystical attraction leads to a physical affair that can last only as long as it takes for him to complete his assignment and move on, but the power of their emotional intimacy lasts a lifetime. In a letter to her children, which she had left for them to read after her death, Francesca explained:

> *The paradox is this: If it hadn't been for Robert Kincaid, I'm not sure I could have stayed on the farm all these years. . . .*
> *In any case, I'm certainly not ashamed of what Robert Kincaid and*

I had together. On the contrary. I loved him desperately throughout all these years. . . . In his own way, through me, he was good to you.

> *Go well, my children.*
> *Mother*

At the end of all this I feel a certain profound sadness. The fictional Francesca, like the real women we have met, is neither a heroine nor a harlot. Rather, her story and those of the women I interviewed combine to underscore the fact that girls who are conditioned to be trusting, accepting, acquiescing people don't realize until far too late that the trade-off for being taken care of by a man is to give up one's very essence.

And yet there is also a certain undeniable joy in these stories. These are not wives who simply make the grim determination to stay in unsatisfying marriages "until death do us part" and then end up as bitter, juiceless old women who spend their senior years inwardly raging because life dealt them a bad hand. On the contrary, the women in this book demonstrate that it is possible to have a fierce drive to make a marriage work and, most of all, to protect children from divorce and yet to have an equally fierce drive to flower fully as a person and a sexual being, even if that requires going outside the marriage for the means to do so. And what is truly remarkable is that each woman who invented for herself the long-term affair alternative found—as did Waller's Francesca—that because her body and soul were nurtured by her adjunct love, she in fact grew stronger and more able to love *within* her marriage and to be a far better mother than if she had allowed herself to remain emotionally and sexually stunted.

Of course, as every wife I interviewed pointed out, the long-term lover solution is definitely not the ideal. It is, at best, makeshift, and the women in this book spoke with one voice when they said that their most fervent wish was that their daughters would somehow find their signature selves *before* marriage and bring to their husbands their total and authentic personas, without guilt or apology for the fullness of their sexual desires, or their unique talents and dreams, or their need to be respected and to be cherished. Is that possible? And can husbands be expected to accept such a package without finding their wives' sexuality somehow "bad" and without being threatened by their wives' talents and skills and earning power? Can men be expected to control the urge to cut self-assured women down to size?

I certainly think so, on all counts. After all, many of the women in this book found men who could meet their needs. The problem, however, is that the wives found these men only after they had already married men who *weren't* capable of meeting their needs. But let's not be too quick to blame the husbands. Remember, both the wives and husbands represented here were by and large very young and unformed when they married. By definition, then, the wives who found just the right lovers were different people from the girls they had been as brides. They were thus in a much better position to make an informed choice instead of "falling in love," a phenomenon which as we have seen has no universal definition and is almost always dangerous.

And so? The solution is as old as the Seven Sages of ancient Greece. Sometime around 600 B.C., according to Plutarch, the following piece of irrefutable wisdom was uttered by the Delphic Oracle: "Know thyself." That admonition still holds true today. My personal wish, as this work draws to a close, is that women will increasingly have the courage to give themselves the luxury of time, and with it the grueling work of introspection, before they march down the aisle.

Yet I also know that given the vagaries of individual lives, many women who do find themselves in marriages with empty spaces will not deny themselves the love they need and deserve, even if they must form secret lives in order to fill up the holes. On some level beyond reason and laws and religious teachings, these women know that when a wife and mother is incomplete, she is not the only one to suffer. Her husband and children become victims of her unfinished psychosexual life as well. Yet the women also know that divorce is a notoriously bad bargain for all concerned. That is why the women choose what they believe to be a kinder solution, forming secret lives with lovers who give them the vigor and self-esteem and sexual satisfaction they need in order to carry out the demands of marriages made when they were too young, too frightened, and too shortsighted to be making a commitment meant to last a lifetime. Thus it is that these women with secret loves—women I have come to know and genuinely respect—feel that they are neither "cheating on" nor in any way cheating their husbands. Quite the opposite, in fact; each wife believes that her lover's love enriches not only her but her family as well. This is because she comes home to share with her husband and children the bountiful spoils of a love relationship that has done for her what her marriage alone could not. She believes her secret life, instead of taking anything away from her family, has allowed her to become all she can be and, therefore, to be a better person for all the people she loves.

Who are we to say otherwise?

Bibliography

Atwater, Lynn, Ph.D. *The Extramarital Connection: Sex, Intimacy, and Identity.* New York: Irvington, 1982.

Atwater, Lynn, Ph.D. "Getting Involved: Women's Transition to First Extramarital Sex." *Alternative Lifestyles* (Sage Publications) 2, no. 1 (February 1979): 33–68.

Becker, Nickie. "Motives for Sexual Infidelity and Its Subsequent Effects on a Marriage." Jackson, Miss.: Mid South Sociological Association, Midwestern State University, November 1978.

Bernard, Jessie. *The Future of Marriage.* New York: Bantam, 1972.

Bianchi, Suzanne M., and Daphne Spain. *American Women in Transition.* New York: Russell Sage Foundation, 1986.

"Breaking the Divorce Cycle." *Newsweek* (January 13, 1992): 48–53.

Cuber, John F., and Peggy B. Harroff. *The Significant Americans.* New York: Appleton-Century-Crofts, 1965.

Ellis, Albert. "Healthy and Disturbed Reasons for Having Extramarital Relations." In *Extramarital Relations,* edited by Gerhard Neubeck, 153–61. Englewood Cliffs, N.J.: Prentice-Hall, 1969.

Fisher, Helen E. *Anatomy of Love: The Natural History of Monogamy, Adultery, and Divorce.* New York: W. W. Norton & Company, 1992.

Friedan, Betty. *The Feminine Mystique.* New York: W. W. Norton, 1963.

Gilman, Charlotte Perkins. *Herland.* New York: Pantheon Books, 1979.

———. "The Yellow Wallpaper," from *The Charlotte Perkins Gilman Reader: "The Yellow Wallpaper" and Other Fiction.* Ann J. Lane, editor. New York: Pantheon Books, 1980.

Greens, Bernard L., M.D., Ronald R. Lee, Ph.D., and Noel Lustig, M.D. "Conscious and Unconscious factors in Marital Infidelity." *Medical Aspects of Human Sexuality* 8, no. 9 (September 1974): 87–111.

Heyn, Dalma. *The Erotic Silence of the American Wife.* New York: Turtle Bay, 1992.

Hunt, Morton. *The Affair.* New York: New American Library, 1969.

Jong, Erica. *Fear of Flying.* New York: Holt, Rinehart and Winston, 1973.

Kean, Sam. *Fire in the Belly.* New York: Bantam Books, 1991.

Lawson, Annette. *Adultery: An Analysis of Love and Betrayal.* New York: Basic Books, 1988.

Lerner, Harriett Goldhor, Ph.D. *Dance of Intimacy.* New York: Harper and Row, 1989.

"Lite Romance." *Los Angeles Times Magazine* (June 14, 1987): 8, 11–14, 16, 36.

Lynch, James J., Ph.D. *The Broken Heart: The Medical Consequences of Loneliness.* New York: Basic Books, 1977.

———. *The Language of the Heart: The Body's Response to Human Dialogue.* New York: Basic Books, 1985.

Meade, Marion. "The Adulterous Wife—Who's She Looking For?" *Sexology* 42, no. 6 (January 1976): 45–49.

Meade, Marion. "Why Wives Commit Adultery: 4 Case Histories." *Sexology* 40, issue F (February 1974), 54–58.

Merck Manual of Diagnosis and Therapy, Sixteenth Edition, Rahway: Merick Research Laboratories, 1992.

Money, John, Ph.D. *Love & Love Sickness: The Science of Sex, Gender Difference, and Pairbonding*. Baltimore and London: Johns Hopkins University Press, 1980.

———. *Lovemaps*. New York: Irvington Publishers, Inc., 1986; Buffalo, N.Y.: Prometheus Books, 1986.

———, and Dr. Margaret Lamacy. *Vandalized Lovemaps*. Buffalo, N.Y.: Prometheus Books, 1989.

———, and Patricia Tucker. *Sexual Signatures on Being a Man or a Woman*. Canada: Little Brown & Co, 1975.

Moulton, Ruth, M.D. "Women with Double Lives." *Contemporary Psychoanalysis* 13, no. 1 (January 1977): 64–84.

The Mythology of All Races. New York: Cooper Square Publishers, 1964.

Oliker, Stacey, Ph.D. *Best Friends and Marriage*. Berkeley: University of California Press, 1989.

Patterson, James, and Peter Kim. *The Day America Told the Truth*. New York: Prentice Hall, 1991.

Pitman, Frank. *Private Lies*. New York: W. W. Norton, 1990.

Ramey, James. *Intimate Friendship*. Englewood Cliffs: Prentice-Hall, 1976.

Sandlin, Joann D. "Extramarital Sex: A Multifaceted Experience." In *Women's Sexual Experience*, edited by M. Kirkpatrick, 239–45 New York: Plenum, 1982.

Strean, Herbert S. "The Extramarital Affair: A Psychoanalytic View." *Psychoanalytic Review* 63, no. 1 (Spring 1976): 103–113.

Tannahill, Reay. *Sex in History*. New York: Stein and Day, 1980.

Tennow, Dorothy. *Love and Limmerance*. New York: Stein and Day, 1979.

Waller, Robert James. *The Bridges of Madison County*. New York: Warner Books, 1992.

Wetzler, Scott, Ph.D. *Living with the Passive-Agressive Man*. New York: Simon & Schuster, 1992.

Wolfe, Linda. *Playing Around: Women and Extramarital Sex*. New York: Morrow, 1975.